Cooking without Looking

VICKI GABEREAU

Cooking without Looking

DOUGLAS & McINTYRE
VANCOUVER/TORONTO

Douglas & McIntyre
1615 Venables Street
Vancouver, British Columbia V5L 2H1

Canadian Cataloguing in Publication Data
Gabereau, Vicki.
Cooking without looking
ISBN 1-55054-151-X
1. Cookery. I. Title.
TX714.G32 1994   641.5   C94-910444-2

Editing by Saeko Usukawa
Illustrations by Robyn Huth
Cover photo design by Rose Cowles
Cover and book design by Praxis
Cover photograph by Philippe Martin-Morice
Printed and bound in Canada by
Best Gagné Book Manufacturers, Inc.
Printed on acid-free paper

Contents

A Word About
Street Kids International

My proceeds from the sales of Cooking without Looking will go to Street Kids International. I want to support their approach—encouraging independence and self-respect through gentle leadership and assistance—to solving problems that seem insurmountable.

Street Kids International was inspired by Peter Dalglish's time spent in Khartoum, Sudan, with UNICEF in 1986. He and a small brigade of youngsters began a bicycle courier service, which is now self-supporting. A similar setup is flourishing in Bangalore, India, and a shoeshine co-operative in Santo Domingo, Dominican Republic is in good shape (in fact, the street kids there have recently branched out into hydroponic market gardening).

Street Kids International, in league with the National Film Board of Canada, has produced a series of animated videos, Karate Kids, directed at HIV/AIDS and substance abuse education. These tapes are now available in twenty-five languages and are distributed the world over.

Donations to Street Kids International are tax deductible.

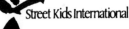
Street Kids International

Street Kids International
56 The Esplanade,
Suite 202
Toronto, Ontario
M5E 1A7

For Tom Rowe

Introduction

Cooking without Looking *is the happy result of six years of recipe exchange on the airwaves. Thousands of requests for the concoctions of expert chefs, famous cookbook authors—and you cooking enthusiasts who listen to CBC Radio in the afternoon—have made this book necessary. When we (the crew, that is, not the royal "we") noticed the mailroom was having to deliver your requests by the bagful, on a cart, it was clear that what the world really needed was another cookbook.*

When I announced to friends and family that I would be preparing a cookbook, most of them could not conceal their puzzlement, knowing as they do that my culinary inspiration and enthusiasm comes from the comedian Gracie Allen (late wife of George Burns). She approached the roasting of a beef thusly: "I buy two roasts, a big one and a little one. And when the little one is burned, the big one is done." Quirky yet reasonable.

She had her way of being in the kitchen, and I have mine. The only bad feature of cooking is the cleaning up bits. I don't fancy that part of the operation and avoid it all costs. I find that inviting strong youths who will be grateful for feeding is a good solution: the proviso is that a little scrubbing of pots while I have a small after-dinner port would be appreciated.

Looking back, six national recipe contests have produced some comical radio moments and several unfounded accusations the fix was in—just because for two years running, the recipe I happened to prepare was judged the winner. These were Groundnut Stew (sent in by a couple who had lived in Africa) and a meat loaf recipe to which I added way more garlic than the directions called for. So I adjusted them a little—I guess I'm somewhat competitive.

Competitive maybe, organized maybe not. But Sheila Peacock, producer of great merit, is. Organized like nothing you've ever seen. She is a miracle, with files forever. Sheila has helmed the cooking features (among other duties) for some years and kept notes and files on every amateur and professional activity on the show that shamelessly carries my name.

Preparing food for a radio broadcast carries with it the odd hitch. Many items are actually cooked right in exciting Studio 23, which is approximately the size of a bathtub. It is a wonder that our permanent technician, Denis Grenier, who is often required to work through vats of this and that to find a microphone cable, doesn't run screaming into the hallway. I think he did, but only once.

This cookbook is full of recipes from around the world and right next door. The selection is what you might call eclectic. A friend of mine, who happens to be a caterer, says that she considers a cookbook a hit if she can find two recipes in it to love and use for years. I hope you'll find at least twenty, maybe even all of them, to your liking. May this little cookbook stay in your kitchen for a long time.

Thanks, eh!

To Sheila Peacock, who did everything, and Julia McKinnell, who thought this cookbook would be a swell idea . . . and Saeko Usukawa, who was patient (that's an understatement). Not to mention the crew on my show would be fatal. Besides, I love them, and they are my closest friends: Rosemary Allenbach, Heather Kennedy, Bill Richardson, Denis Grenier, Karin Konstantynowicz, Evan Stewart, Doug Tuck, Rochelle Collins, Deb Smith, Meredith Levine, Marg Meikle, John Dritmanis, David Grierson.

Cooking without Looking

1

Simple and Comforting

My Favourite Cider and Honey-Glazed Ribs

In Waterloo Region we have no use for spareribs. We have thick, meaty ribs, not spare ones. These are easy to prepare and divine to eat.

2 to 3	strips of ribs (enough for 6)	2 to 3
3 cups	cider	750 mL
1/2 cup	honey	125 mL
2 Tbsp.	lemon juice	30 mL
2 tsp.	sage	10 mL
1 1/2 tsp.	dry mustard	7 mL
1 tsp.	thyme	5 mL
	Salt	

1 Spread the ribs in a large shallow pan. Blend all the other ingredients and pour over the meat. Marinate in a cold place for several hours or overnight. Turn the ribs occasionally.

2 Take the ribs from the pan but save the marinade. Spread the ribs in a large baking pan—the less they overlap the better. Bake at 350°F (180°C); set your timer for 20 minutes, then generously baste the meat with the marinade. Baste every 20 minutes for 1 1/2 hours, or until the ribs are tender and the marinade has turned into an irresistible glaze. Of course, ribs should be served with boiled, mashed, or baked potatoes and sauerkraut, but other vegetables will do.

As a child (okay, I was nineteen), I was sent in remittance-like fashion to live with friends of my parents. This was no ordinary family; certainly nothing like the deadly quiet family I'd grown up in. These people were Bertons, as in Pierre and Janet. They had legions of children and many many parties to celebrate almost anything.

Soon after my arrival, one such wild event was scheduled. It was there that I first met Edna Staebler, one of this country's finest food writers and cookbook authors, including the Schmecks Appeal series. It didn't take me long to discover the reason for her great celebrity, especially in the kitchen of Janet Berton, a mad-keen cook herself. Ms. Staebler's cookbooks continue to be the backbone and inspiration for many North American chefs, professional and not so professional.

Schnippled Bean Salad (Frenched Bean Salad)

1 quart	green (or yellow) string beans	1 L
1	smallish onion	1
	Salt	

Dressing:

1 tsp.	sugar	5 mL
1 tsp.	vinegar	5 mL
1/2 tsp.	salt	2 mL
	Pepper	
3/4 cup	sour cream	175 mL

1 Cut the stems off the beans, wash them, then schnipple them—that means cutting the beans on a slant in very thin slices, one bean being cut into 3 or 4 long slices. (Or you could use frozen frenched beans.) Put the beans into boiling salted water and cook them just long enough to be barely soft. Drain and cool them.

2 Meantime, peel and slice the onion and sprinkle it liberally with salt and stir it around; let it stand at least 15 minutes, giving it a stir now and then.

3 In a bowl large enough to contain the beans, put the sugar, vinegar, 1/2 teaspoon (2 mL) salt, a good sprinkling of pepper, and sour cream. Stir all together.

4 Now take the salted onion into your hand and with the other hand squeeze as much of the juice out of it as you can. Put the squeezed onion into the dressing, pour the drained beans into the bowl and mix with the dressing till all the beans are generously coated—you might need more cream.

Speedy Pat-in Pastry

Because pie plates vary in size, you may have to adjust the recipe. Most recipes are for 9-inch (23-cm) pies.

1 1/2 cups	flour	375 mL
1 1/2 tsp.	sugar	7 mL
3/4 tsp.	salt	4 mL
1/2 cup	oil	125 mL
3 Tbsp.	cold milk	45 mL

1 Sift the flour, sugar and salt directly into a 9-inch (23-cm) pie plate or into your food processor.

2 Combine the oil and milk; beat with a fork until creamy. Pour all at once over the flour; give your processor a brief whirl—or in the pie plate mix with a fork until the flour is completely dampened.

3 Pat the dough with your fingers to line the sides and bottom of the pie plate. Flute the edges, then fill with whatever filling you've chosen. If you're making a baked shell to be filled later, prick the entire surface of the pastry with a fork to keep it from bubbling. Bake at 425°F (220°C) for 15 minutes until golden.

Fluffy Pumpkin Pie

I have a fairly deep pie plate but I find that the filling sometimes fluffs up and I have more than I need to fill it; if that happens, I quickly pat in a bit more pastry and make another small pie—or put the overflow into a buttered custard dish to be baked and served as a pudding. Of course, I prefer seeing whipped cream heaped over the top of pumpkin pie when I serve it—but I find it is safer to put a bowl of whipped cream on the table to let people help themselves. It is unlikely that you'll have any pie left over, but if you do it's better not to have the cream melting on top—especially if you might like to have the pie for breakfast next morning, or—as I often do—two healthy wedges for lunch. After all, pumpkin is a vegetable.

Pastry for a 9-inch (23-cm) pie

2 cups	cooked and puréed pumpkin	500 mL
1/2 cup or less	milk	125 mL or less
3	eggs, separated	3
1	cup sugar	250 mL
1/2 tsp.	cinnamon	2 mL
1/4 tsp.	cloves	1 mL
1/4 tsp.	nutmeg	1 mL
1/2 tsp.	salt	2 mL
1 tsp.	vanilla	5 mL

1 Mix the pumpkin and milk, beaten egg yolks, then the sugar mixed with the spices, salt and vanilla. Fold in the stiffly beaten egg whites, turn the mixture into the unbaked pie shell, and bake about 45 minutes in a 350°F (180°C) oven.

Serves 6 to 8.

Grandma's Famous Bannock

2 cups	lukewarm water	500 mL
2 tsp.	salt	10 mL
2 Tbsp.	sugar	25 mL
2 Tbsp.	vegetable oil	25 mL
1 1/2 tsp.	instant yeast	7 mL
6–6 1/2	cups flour	1.5–1.75 L
	Vegetable oil for frying	

1 In a large bowl, combine lukewarm water, salt, sugar, oil and yeast. Add 6 cups (1.5 L) flour, mixing by hand when dough becomes stiff.

2 Turn dough out onto lightly floured surface. Knead for 10 minutes or until smooth and elastic. Let rise for 1 1/2 hours. Punch down.

3 Pat dough into 12 x 18-inch (30 x 45-cm) oblong. Cut into 2-inch (5-cm) wide strips. Cut strips into 2-inch (5-cm) squares. Flatten squares very gently with the palm of your hand.

4 In a large heavy frypan, heat 1 inch (2.5 cm) of oil over high heat to 375°F (190°C) or until a small piece of dough floats. Fry until golden brown, about 5 minutes, turning bannock over halfway through frying.

Variations

Raisin Bannock: Add 1 cup of raisins with the flour.

Cinnamon Bannock: Combine 1/2 cup (125 mL) packed brown sugar with 2 tablespoons (30 mL) cinnamon. With a knife, spread softened butter on warm cooked bannock and sprinkle with the sugar mixture.

Dolly Watts, a Gitksan from near Hazelton in northern British Columbia, makes just about the best bannock I've ever tasted. It was part of her everyday life while growing up, and it is today too. Ms. Watts and her Vancouver catering company, called Just Like Grandma's Bannock, are in big demand to provide feasts of Northwest Coast indigenous cuisine.

Dolly and I got along like a house on fire, which almost nearly happened. Due the shower-stall-sized studio and the lack of ventilation, most of the oxygen was replaced by vegetable oil fumes. It was bannock to go!

Note: For historical purposes (even though this is a century-old recipe), it can be presumed that Grandma, after whom this recipe is named, never used instant yeast.

Savoury Pecan Loaf

*C*harmaine Solomon is considered one of the top food professionals in the world—Asian and vegetarian being her specialities. Her numerous cookbooks include The Complete Asian Cookbook, Charmaine Solomon's Complete Vegetarian Cookbook and Charmaine Solomon's Thai Cookbook.

It all started on a whim when she entered a cooking contest. The judges went wild over her entry, a biscuit into which she had flung some herbs and a bit of cheese. She has been in the food business ever since—lucky for us.

Serve this high-protein loaf with cooked vegetables or a green salad.

8 oz.	pecan kernels	250 g
3 cups	fresh wholegrain bread crumbs	750 mL
2 Tbsp.	butter (or oil)	30 mL
1 cup	finely chopped onions	250 mL
1 cup	finely chopped celery	250 mL
1 cup	finely grated carrot	250 mL
1 cup	cottage cheese (optional)	250 mL
1 tsp.	dried oregano	5 mL
3	eggs, beaten	3
1 tsp.	salt	5 mL
1/2 tsp.	pepper	2 mL
1/2 cup	chopped parsley	125 mL

1 Finely chop the pecans—a food processor does this quickly. Combine in a bowl with the bread crumbs.

2 Heat the butter or oil and cook the onions over medium heat until soft and golden. Remove from heat, add to the pecans together with the rest of the ingredients and mix thoroughly.

3 Put into a greased loaf tin and bake in an oven preheated to 350°F (180°C) for 35 to 40 minutes or until firm.

Serves 6.

HOUSEHOLD HINTS
To clean the leaves of household plants, dampen a clean soft cloth with room-temperature milk. Wipe each leaf individually. Your plants will have a wonderful sheen.
—LISA J. IZSO
OF CALGARY, ALBERTA

Country Captain

3 lb.	chicken (or chicken pieces)	1.5 kg
2	cloves garlic, crushed	2
2 tsp.	salt	10 mL
1 tsp.	ground turmeric	5 mL
1/2 tsp.	ground black pepper	2 mL
4 Tbsp.	oil	50 mL
4	large onions, thinly sliced	4
2	fresh red chilies, seeded and sliced	2
1/2 cup	water	125 mL

1 Cut chicken into serving pieces. Combine garlic, salt, turmeric, pepper and rub well into chicken.

2 Heat oil in a large saucepan and gently fry half the sliced onion until brown. Remove onion from pan and set aside.

3 Fry remaining onion and chilies until just starting to colour, then add chicken to pan and fry until golden all over. Add water, cover and simmer gently until chicken is tender. Uncover and continue to simmer, allowing any liquid remaining in pan to evaporate.

4 Serve hot, garnished with the reserved fried onion and accompanied by fried potatoes or ghee rice.

Serves 6.

When she came to my studio in Vancouver, she was on a North American tour, cooking and talking to delighted throngs. Just in passing, she gave a little quiz: "How do you say this word: basil?"

"Basil," I said, "as in Basil Rathbone, not 'baysil,' and don't let them tell you otherwise. Next question."

"Cumin," she shouted. "How do you say that, then?"

"Cumin," I said, "as in 'qumin.'"

"Wrong," she said, "it's 'cumin' like 'she'll be cumin around the mountain.'"

We laughed and screamed. I was enlightened.

Then there's turmeric. Don't forget that r. Here endeth the lesson.

Puttanesca (Pasta of the Night)

D iane Clement has written four cookbooks, all "on the run"—Chef on the Run, Doctor and Chef on the Run—you get the idea. She's also the co-owner of the Tomato Fresh Food Cafe in Vancouver. In her youth, Diane and her husband, Dr. Doug, were first-rate athletes, competing in the Commonwealth Games, the Olympics, etc. They were and are still in top condition. They never stop running and they never stop eating. Tells you something, doesn't it!

Diane has an unusual voice, as if she'd shouted at a hockey game for the entire three periods. She does not go unmissed in a crowd and is therefore great entertainment in life and on the radio. When she's on the air, you know it.

You must not leave out the anchovies—they are an essential element. The fish taste disappears in the cooking and even anchovy haters won't be able to tell. One other thing about anchovies—use them immediately after opening the tin. Don't let them sit around for too long as they get funky, which is why so many people hate them.

If you are in a huge hurry, you can simply chop up all the tomato mixture ingredients, throw them into a large heavy skillet, simmer for 10 to 15 minutes, and carry on with the rest of the recipe.

8 to 10	medium tomatoes, in 1/2 inch (1 cm) slices	8 to 10
2 sm cans	anchovies, drained, patted dry and chopped	2 sm cans
1/2 cup or more	black pitted olives, chopped	125 mL or more
5 or more	cloves garlic, finely chopped	5 or more
1/2 tsp.	dried crushed red pepper flakes	2 mL
1 cup or more	fresh basil	250 mL or more
	Olive oil	
1–11/2 lbs.	dried spaghetti (or penne or fettuccine)	500–750 g
1 cup	freshly grated Parmigiano-Reggiano (or asiago) Freshly ground black pepper	250 mL

1. Preheat oven to 350°F (180°C).

2. In a large lasagne-type pan about 12 x 15 inches (30 x 38 cm), make two layers each of the tomatoes, anchovies, olives, garlic, pepper flakes and 1/2 cup (125 mL) of the basil, in that order. Drizzle each layer well with olive oil and a good sprinkling of black pepper. Bake for 30 to 35 minutes.

3. In the meantime, cook the pasta. Drain and put in a large serving bowl and toss with a little bit of olive oil and half of the cheese. Chop up the baked tomato mixture and add to the pasta. Add the rest of the cheese and the rest of the basil.

4. Serve with crusty Italian bread to mop up the juice, and offer more grated cheese and black pepper to taste.

Serves 6.

Over the years, Diane has provided scores of recipes for the happy listener, but the one I prepare the most often is Puttanesca. This is a bone-simple pasta recipe that tastes so good you won't believe you made it yourself. It's a quickie, too, which is the reason it was developed in the first place. Ladies of the night in Siena found it a boon to time management.

Spicy Nuts

T he Spicy Nuts
are as addictive a
little savoury as I can
imagine, and they
make great gifts at
Christmas too.

2	cloves garlic, crushed	2
3 Tbsp.	butter	45 mL
3 Tbsp.	Worcestershire sauce	45 mL
1/2 tsp. or more	cinnamon	2 mL or more
1/4 tsp. or more	cayenne pepper	1 mL or more
few drops	Tabasco sauce	few drops
4 cups	nuts (pecans, almonds, cashews, one of a kind or in combination)	1 L

1 Preheat oven to 300°F (150°C).

2 Mix garlic and butter. In a heavy skillet, combine the butter mixture, Worcestershire sauce, cinnamon, cayenne pepper and Tabasco. Simmer for a few minutes, then add the nuts and toss well.

3 Spread the nuts on a cookie sheet and bake for about 10 minutes. Turn the nuts over and bake for another 5 to 10 minutes, or until slightly brown and crisp. Cool. Store in an airtight container or freeze.

Vicki's Crème Brûlée

3 cups	whipping cream	750 mL
5 Tbsp.	sugar	65 mL
1 Tbsp.	vanilla	15 mL
8	egg yolks	8
1/4 cup	golden brown sugar	50 mL
	Garnish of strawberries	
	(or raspberries)	

1 Preheat oven to 325°F (160°C).

2 In a double boiler over simmering water, combine whipping cream and sugar. Heat until the sugar dissolves and the mixture is hot to the touch. Add the vanilla.

3 In a large mixing bowl, beat the egg yolks until thick. Slowly add the hot whipping cream mixture, stirring constantly. Pour the mixture into a 9-inch (23-cm) square deep dish, an ovenproof glass pie pan or individual custard cups. Set the dish in a larger baking pan and add enough hot water to reach halfway up the sides of the dish holding the custard.

4 Bake for 35 to 40 minutes or until the custard is set and a knife inserted comes out clean. It should have the consistency of *soft* yogurt. Cool, then refrigerate. Can be made to this stage a day ahead.

5 Several hours before serving, press brown sugar though a sieve onto the custard to form an even 1/4 inch (5 mm) layer. Broil 4 inches (10 cm) from the heat for about 1 minute, until the sugar begins to melt and bubble. Watch closely to prevent burning. Chill. Just before serving, garnish with berries.

Serves 6 to 8.

I 've changed the name of Diane's Crème Brûlée to Vicki's Crème Brûlée because it's my favourite dessert. I rarely make it because, well, it's just too—well, you know— it makes you fat immediately. But for our purposes, and once or twice a year, you just gotta! There are a couple of tricks to this recipe: don't put the brown sugar on the custard until you are ready to serve it and don't think you can just whip this up ten minutes before dinner. It's way better to make it the day before. Although this makes enough to serve six to eight people, most of us would eat two portions if presented with the opportunity and if you lie about the whipping cream.

Magnificent Chicken Pie

In the 1950s, Evelyn Birkby, a farmwife from Mill Creek valley in southwestern Iowa, became a radio homemaker. Thousands of women who shared the same kind of workload tuned in daily to hear all the latest domestic science. Radio programs like "Down a Country Lane" (and her newspaper column, which was "Up a Country Lane") just don't exist any more. Her cookbooks are Neighboring on the Air: Cooking with the KMA Radio Homemakers and Up a Country Lane Cookbook.

1	stewing chicken (or large fryer)	1
6 Tbsp.	butter (or margarine)	75 mL
12	small onions	12
7 Tbsp.	flour	100 mL
	Salt and pepper to taste	
	Dash of mace	
1/2 tsp.	Worcestershire sauce	2 mL
1 cup	milk (or half-and-half)	250 mL
2 cups	chicken broth	500 mL

1 Cover chicken with water and simmer, covered, until tender, 1 to 2 hours. Cool. Remove skin and bones and cut meat into bite-sized pieces. Place in 9 x 13-inch (22 x 34-cm) baking pan.

2 In a skillet, sauté onions in butter or margarine. With a slotted spoon, lift onions from skillet and spoon over the chicken.

3 Blend flour into drippings in skillet, add seasonings and Worcestershire sauce and gradually stir in milk or half-and-half and chicken broth. Cook, stirring, until mixture is thickened.

4 Pour gravy over chicken and onion layers. Put in a 400°F (200°C) oven to keep hot while you prepare the biscuits.

Makes about 8 servings.

Carrot Biscuits

2 cups	biscuit mix (or make your own— see recipe on page 16)	500 mL
1/2 cup	coarsely grated raw carrots	125 mL
	Milk to make a soft dough	

see recipe on page 16

1 Combine ingredients. Roll out the dough and cut into rings with a doughnut cutter so each biscuit has a hole in the centre. If you want larger biscuits or don't have a doughnut cutter, use a can as a cutter for the circle and a lid from a catsup or other bottle to make the centre hole.

2 Arrange biscuit rings on top of the chicken in the casserole. Brush tops with milk. Bake 15 to 20 minutes at 425° F (220°C) or until light brown.

3 Meanwhile, cook 1 cup (250 mL) of fresh peas or 1 package of frozen peas with a little water added or heat 1 can of peas. Drain. Season the peas and put a heaping spoonful in the centre of each biscuit ring. Any remaining peas can be served in a separate dish.

When Mrs. Birkby was a guest (twice) on the show, even just the tone of her voice reminded me of the kind of radio, Canadian and American, that kept us so cosily glued together. People in this country who heard her know why she was so loved in hers.

Real Country Biscuits

2 cups	flour	500 mL
3/4 tsp.	salt	4 mL
1 Tbsp.	baking powder	15 mL
1/4 cup	shortening	50 mL
1/4 tsp.	baking soda	1 mL
1 cup	buttermilk	250 mL

1 Sift first three ingredients into bowl. Cut in shortening until mixture is like coarse bread crumbs. (Lard makes light, tender biscuits just as it does pie crust, but homogenized shortening like Crisco is also excellent.)

2 Combine baking soda with buttermilk. Blend into dry ingredients with fork. When barely moistened, turn out on floured breadboard and knead a few times. Pat out to about 1/2 inch (1 cm) thick and cut into rounds.

3 Bake on a greased cookie sheet at 425°F (220°C) for 10 to 12 minutes or until brown. This is a fine recipe to use with Carrot Biscuits recipe on page 15.

Makes about 1 dozen biscuits, depending on size.

HOUSEHOLD HINTS
To clean the glass doors on a wood stove, dip a damp cloth in the ashes and wipe all over the windows. Then wipe clean with newspapers. Presto!

—VIRGINIA FOLEY OF BOWMANVILLE, ONTARIO

Vegetable Bisque

3/4 cup	diced carrots	175 mL
1 cup	thinly sliced leeks	250 mL
1 cup	diced potato	250 mL
1 3/4 cups	chicken stock	425 mL
1/4 cup	chopped parsley	50 mL
1/4 cup	2 per cent milk	50 mL
	Dash each salt, pepper and nutmeg	
	Thinly sliced green onion	
	(or chopped chives)	
	Thin strips process cheese slices	

S ort of retired now, after twenty years of writing a food column for Weekend Magazine and Today, Margo Oliver has turned her attention to people of a certain age who find themselves cooking for one. That certain age can be seventy-five in a condo, or eighteen in a college dorm. Her books are Good Food for One and Cookbook for Seniors. Here is her hearty (and healthy) soup.

1 Combine carrots, leeks, potato and chicken stock in a medium saucepan. Bring to a boil, reduce heat, cover, and simmer until vegetables are tender, about 15 minutes. Add parsley and simmer 2 minutes.

2 Pour into the blender and blend until smooth. Return to saucepan, add milk and heat well. Taste and season with salt, pepper and nutmeg. Ladle into bowl and top with green onion (or chives) and a few strips of cheese.

To microwave: Combine carrots, leeks, potato, and chicken stock in a 2-quart (2-L) casserole. Cover and cook at high about 12 minutes, until vegetables are tender. Stir once or twice. Add parsley and cook, covered, 30 seconds. Complete as above, reheating in serving bowl in microwave.

Makes 2 generous servings.

Broccoli- or Cauliflower-Cheese Soup

U nlike many cookbook authors, James McNair focusses on one thing at a time. What a good idea! Pizza, for instance, or the potato, or salmon, or cheese— each has an entire book devoted to its preparation. McNair is a purist, so when he lifted this soup recipe from his Aunt Doris, he substituted real Cheddar and Emmentaler for the processed cheese, and homemade chicken broth with mushrooms for the canned mushroom soup. The result! Perfection.

1 lb.	broccoli (or cauliflower), coarsely chopped	500 g
6 Tbsp.	(3/4 stick) unsalted butter	90 mL
1/4 cup	all-purpose flour	50 mL
4 cups	poultry stock (or canned chicken broth, preferably low-salt type)	1 L
2 cups	heavy (whipping) cream (or light cream or half-and-half)	500 mL
	Salt	
	Freshly ground black pepper	
1 cup	chopped yellow onion	250 mL
1 Tbsp.	minced or pressed garlic	15 mL
1/2 lb.	fresh mushrooms, chopped	250 g
3 Tbsp.	minced fresh (or canned) jalapeño chilies, or to taste	40 mL
1 cup	freshly shredded Cheddar cheese, about 3 oz. (85 g)	250 mL
1 cup	freshly shredded Emmentaler (or Jarlsberg) cheese, about 3 oz. (85 g)	250 mL
	Slivered baked ham for garnish	

1 Place the broccoli or cauliflower in a steamer rack set over simmering water, cover, and steam until just tender, about 6 minutes. Remove from heat, rinse with cold water to stop the cooking and preserve colour, and drain. Chop finely and set aside.

2 In a soup pot or large, heavy saucepan, melt 3 table-spoons (45 mL) of the butter over low heat. Add the flour and cook, stirring constantly, for about 3 minutes. Whisk in the stock or broth and cream or half-and-half. Increase the heat to medium-high and bring to a boil, stirring or whisking constantly. Reduce the heat to low and simmer, stirring occasionally, until thickened, about 10 minutes. Season to taste with salt and pepper.

3 Meanwhile, in a sauté pan or skillet, heat the remaining 3 tablespoons (45 mL) butter over low heat. Add the onion and sauté until soft but not golden, about 8 minutes. Add the garlic, mushrooms, and chilies and sauté until the mushrooms are soft, about 5 minutes longer. Transfer to the cream mixture. Add the broccoli or cauliflower and the cheeses and cook over low heat, stirring almost constantly, until cheese melts, about 5 minutes; do not allow to approach a boil. Season to taste with salt and pepper.

4 Ladle into preheated bowls, garnish with the ham, and serve hot. Alternatively, pour into a container and refrigerate, uncovered, until cool, then tightly cover and store up to 3 days. Slowly reheat, stirring frequently to keep cheese from curdling, before garnishing and serving.

Serves 6 to 8 as a soup course, or 3 or 4 as a main dish.

HOUSEHOLD HINTS

To clean the copper bottoms of pots and pans, spread a layer of tomato soup directly from the can onto the copper. Let it sit for one to two hours and then rinse in hot water. The copper will be shiny clean.

—VALERIE BUCHAN
OF YARKER, ONTARIO

Vichyssoise

I love vichyssoise more than I love my car, though my car is a lot less trouble. The last time I made vichyssoise, it was a disaster. I tripled the recipe so that I could feed many people. Then I put the prepared liquid, which had taken hours to make, into glass containers when it was still too hot and put them in the fridge. The glass cracked. All was lost. I've since found an easier recipe—this one from Winter Pleasures—Herbs and Comfort Cooking. And I'm not as stupid (that's debatable).

Traditionally made with leeks, I have often substituted onions and shallots in vichyssoise. Instead of the usual cream, I have found milk quite satisfactory. The soup still has a creamy texture but has less fat.

2 cups	washed and finely chopped leeks	500 mL
4 Tbsp.	butter (or margarine)	60 mL
8 cups	potatoes, peeled and sliced	2 L
6 cups	chicken stock	1.5 L
4 cups	2 per cent milk (or cream)	1 L
	Freshly ground pepper	
	Dash of nutmeg	
	Chopped chives (or parsley	
	or green onions) as garnish	

1 In a large saucepan, sauté the washed, chopped leeks in the butter or margarine until soft (about 5 minutes).

2 Add potatoes and chicken stock to the leeks and simmer for 20 minutes, until potatoes are soft.

3 Purée the soup in batches in the food processor. Return it to the saucepan and add the milk, pepper and nutmeg. Sprinkle soup with chopped herbs and serve hot in winter or cold in summer.

Serves 6 to 8.

Jurgen's Pork Chop Surprise

	Pork chops	
	Homemade sauerkraut	
	Juniper berries	
	Caraway	
2 oz.	gin	60 mL
	Pepper	
	Slices of apple (optional)	

1 Preheat oven to 375°F (190°C).

2 Put all the ingredients in a baking dish and cover. Bake for 30 to 35 minutes, then 5 minutes with the lid off.

J urgen Gothe, whose show "Disc Drive" is broadcast opposite mine on the CBC Stereo network, is a swell guy, except that he can't remember ever giving me this recipe, let alone his appearance on my show to describe it. That is why I've added the word "surprise" to his, or not his, recipe. It's sure to surprise somebody.

You will notice that there are no quantities divulged except, of course, the gin. And you really ought to feel free to change that too. Just don't call me in the middle of the night and ask "Whadda I do now?" Call Jurgen.

By the way, he's also the host of "The Cooking Game" show on television.

HOUSEHOLD HINTS

On the occasion of a friend's marriage, my friend's mother told her: "When you've been out a little late in the afternoon and you don't have anything ready for his supper, throw on some lipstick and quickly chop some onions into a frying pan with butter. Then when you greet him at the door, he'll smell the onions cooking and that will buy you some time."

—TOBY YULL OF HAMILTON, ONTARIO

Shepherd's Pie

James Barber is host of the wonderfully successful television cooking show "The Urban Peasant." His kitchen is to be envied—it has all the bells and whistles, and he doesn't have to clean up after himself!

Some years ago, James released a couple of cookbooks called Ginger Tea Makes Friends and Fear of Frying, and in addition to providing the recipes, he made little line drawings showing you how to amalgamate simple ingredients into dishes of remarkable sophistication. My favourite remains his shepherd's pie. He says he's fond of shepherds, but he wouldn't necessarily want his sister to marry one.

6 or 7	medium potatoes, peeled and halved	6 or 7
	Salt and pepper	
	Butter	
2 Tbsp.	oil	30 mL
3	medium onions, chopped	3
1	large carrot, grated	1
1 1/2 lb.	ground beef	750 g
1 1/2 tsp.	rosemary	7 mL
1 tsp.	salt	5 mL
2 tsp.	Worcestershire sauce	10 mL

1 Turn on oven to 425°F (220°C).

2 In a large saucepan, lid on, cook potatoes in boiling salted water till tender, 25 to 30 minutes. Drain and mash with pepper and 4 oz. (125 g) butter.

3 In a frying pan, heat oil and fry onions until transparent. Add grated carrot, ground beef and rosemary. Turn it over a lot; cook just till the meat separates. Add salt and Worcestershire.

4 Butter a casserole. Put in the meat mixture. Cover meat mixture with the mashed potatoes. Dot top with butter. Bake in oven for 15 to 20 minutes, till light brown.

5 Eat with peas.

Serves 5.

Quick Cassoulet

Instead of dry red wine, you may substitute 1/2 cup (125 mL) of chicken broth and 1 tablespoon (15 mL) of red wine vinegar.

1 Tbsp.	vegetable oil	15 mL
4	chicken breast halves, boneless and skinless	4
1/2 lb.	hot Italian sausage, cut in 1/2-inch (1-cm) slices	250 g
3	medium carrots, sliced	3
1	medium onion, sliced	1
1	clove garlic, minced	1
1/2 cup	dry red wine	125 mL
1	bay leaf	1
1 tsp.	dried thyme	5 mL
1/4 tsp.	pepper	1 mL
1 14-oz. can	beans with pork in tomato sauce	1 398-mL can
	Chopped parsley	

1 In a large frying pan, heat the oil over medium-high heat. Brown the chicken and sausage. Add the carrots, onion and garlic; sauté for 2 minutes.

2 Drain off the fat. Stir in the wine, bay leaf, thyme and pepper. Cover and simmer over low heat for about 15 minutes or until the chicken is no longer pink. Stir in the beans and heat through. Sprinkle parsley on top.

Serves 4.

O nce in a while I am asked to make a speech, the text of which usually involves some sort of incoherent rambling about what I do for a living—which is talk. And I should include listen. Actually, listening is the best part. If I fail to listen in my business, I could, with some dispatch, be looking for a new business.

Another point is not to pass up a story that at first glance appears to be not quite as gripping as a paleo-scatologist (you just think about it). When the Canadian Bean Council pitched us bean recipes, I had to think twice, and that, as it turned out, was too long. Their recipe for cassoulet was a huge hit with the crew that ate it and the people who wrote in to get it. This is easy to make, nutritious and has only 447 calories per serving (if you don't inhale the whole pan, as did the aforementioned crew).

Beans 'n' Rice

S till more beans. Public discussion of bodily functions, especially those below the waist, upsets my Victorian soul, but I hate that coyness. So when bean-mad Kay Spicer, a nutritionist, came into the studio, I asked her about the gas challenge. Her response: "More is better. The more you eat them, the better you digest them."

Here is a presentation that is centuries old—the co-starring of beans and rice—and found in many international cuisines. The added cheese comes from Mexican-style beans and rice.

1 tsp.	canola oil	5 mL
1	onion, chopped	1
1	clove garlic, chopped	1
1	tsp. chili powder	5 mL
1/2 tsp.	ground cumin	2 mL
1/4 tsp.	celery seed	1 mL
1/4 tsp.	freshly ground black pepper	1 mL
1 19-oz. can	tomatoes	1 540-mL can
2 cups	cooked red kidney beans	500 mL
1 cup	cooked brown (or white) long-grain rice	250 mL
1 tsp.	Worcestershire sauce	5 mL
1	green sweet pepper, chopped	1
1/2 tsp.	salt	2 mL
1/3 cup	shredded Cheddar cheese	75 mL
	Chopped fresh cilantro (or parsley)	

1 In a large saucepan, heat oil over medium heat; cook onion and garlic, stirring occasionally, for 5 minutes or until onion is translucent. Stir in chili powder, cumin, celery seed and pepper, cook for 1 minute.

2 Add tomatoes, beans, rice and Worcestershire sauce; stir well. Bring to boil, reduce heat and simmer for about 20 minutes or until most of the liquid evaporates.

3 Stir in green pepper. Cook for about 2 minutes or until heated through. Season to taste with salt.

4 Garnish each serving with cheese and cilantro.

Makes 6 servings.

Variation

Cuban Beans and Rice (sometimes called Moors & Christians): In place of kidney beans, use 2 cups (500 mL) cooked black beans.

Tortilla Bean Pinwheels

So get with the program, because with fewer and fewer of us eating meat seven days a week, the lowly legume is finding a bigger place in the Western diet.

1 cup	cooked kidney beans	250 mL
2 tsp.	molasses	10 mL
1 tsp.	chili powder	5 mL
1 tsp.	Dijon mustard	5 mL
Pinch	freshly ground black pepper	Pinch
3 8-inch	tortillas	3 20-cm
1/2 cup	light cream cheese	125 mL
4	green onions, thinly sliced	4

1 In a small bowl or food processor, mash together or process beans, molasses, chili powder, mustard and pepper until smooth.

2 Spread each tortilla with one-third of the cream cheese. Spread bean mixture over cheese. Sprinkle with green onions.

3 Roll up each tortilla, jelly-roll fashion, to make a log. Trim thin ends from each roll. Wrap snugly in plastic wrap or waxed paper. Refrigerate for at least 3 hours or up to 24 hours.

4 At serving time, cut into slices about 1/2 inch (1 cm) thick.

Makes 9 servings (36 pinwheels).

Clams in Coconut Milk

Charles van Sandwyk is a modern-day Gauguin. He spends most of each year living and painting on a remote tropical island called Tavewa, in Fiji. Tavewa has no shops, no roads, no running water, and the nearest phone is two islands away, so you either bring in supplies or you use what's there.

Still a teenager when he left for the South Pacific, he quickly had to learn how to cook, what with no momma and no McDonald's. The residents of his island no doubt stared at him in his adolescent inability to even boil an egg. Things have picked up for our Charles since, and here's his recipe for clams and coconut milk.

1 1/2 lb.	clams	750 g
1	medium-size onion, sliced	1
2	cloves garlic, chopped	2
	Fresh chopped chilies (or chili powder) to taste	
	Salt to taste	
	Juice of half a lime	
1 1/2 cups	(approx) canned coconut milk	375 mL
1/2 cup	water (optional)	125 mL

1 Clean clams and place in bottom of a pot. Top with onion, garlic and chilies. Salt to taste, if desired. Add lime juice. Pour coconut milk over until it just covers the other ingredients. If the broth is too rich for you, add water.

2 Bring pot to a boil, then simmer for 10 minutes. The clamshells should open.

Vegetarian Lasagne

This recipe only looks complicated. Actually, you can play with it—arrange the layers differently, increase the thickness of some and leave out others. For assembly, prepare all the ingredients and have them lined up in front of you.

Boil *in plenty of water until al dente, approximately 7 or 8 minutes. Rinse and drain.*

1 pkg.	lasagne noodles	1pkg.

Mix *in a separate bowl*

2 cups	ricotta cheese	500 mL
2	eggs	2
1/4 cup	grated Parmesan cheese	50 mL

Shred *in a second bowl*

1 cup	mozzarella cheese	250 mL

Fry *over medium heat until soft and place in a third bowl*

1	large eggplant, cubed	1
2	zucchini, cubed	2
1/2	large onion, chopped	1/2
1 tsp.	chopped garlic	5 mL
5 Tbsp.	vegetable oil	75 mL

Layer 1	1/4 28-oz. (796-mL) can tomato sauce in a 9 x 13-inch (23 x 33-cm) pan	
Layer 2	1/4 of the lasagne noodles	
Layer 3	all of the ricotta mixture	
Layer 4	1/4 of the lasagne noodles	
Layer 5	1/4 of the tomato sauce	
Layer 6	1/2 cup mozzarella	125 mL
Layer 7	1/4 of the lasagne noodles	
Layer 8	1/4 of the tomato sauce	
Layer 9	all of the vegetable mixture	
Layer 10	1/4 of the lasagne noodles	
Layer 11	1/4 of the tomato sauce	
Layer 12	1/2 cup mozzarella	125 mL
Layer 13	1/3 cup grated Parmesan cheese	75 mL

Bake *at 350°F (180°C) for 1 hour, remove from oven and let sit 10 to 15 minutes.*

Serves *8 to 10 people. Leftover lasagne freezes well.*

In the same spirit as the Picasso restaurant in Vancouver, the Trinity Square and the Cawthra Square cafes in Toronto were opened to provide work and training for the mentally challenged. They have been great successes, with quality and professionalism consistently maintained. People line up to get their vegetarian lasagne, but you won't have to. Here's the recipe from The Trinity Square and Cawthra Square Cafe Cookbook.

Brie en Croute

S usan Mendelson, the author of many cookbooks (including Mama Never Cooked Like This and Food to Grow On—the latter with her sister, Rena Mendelson) is possibly the most energetic woman I have ever encountered. She zooms. She owns the Lazy Gourmet food store in Vancouver, and there's a certain irony in that name. But she knows how to prepare dishes for those of us who are lazy or in a hurry.

This recipe makes a good party piece, being both impressive and ridiculously easy. I, however, have managed to burn it and have it melt all over the oven, so pay attention to the baking instructions and you'll be fine.

2	pieces purchased frozen puff pastry	2
4 1/2-oz.	of brie, diameter about	125-g
wheel	4 1/2 inches (11.5 cm)	wheel
1/2 cup	peeled apple chunks	125 mL
	Brown sugar	
	Cinnamon	

1 Thaw pastry and roll out in circles.

2 Preheat oven to 400°F (200°C).

3 Place brie on top of a circle of puff pastry. On top of brie, put apple chunks. Sprinkle on brown sugar and cinnamon.

4 Place the other circle of puff pastry on top, crimping the edges.

5 Bake in oven for 15 minutes.

HOUSEHOLD HINTS

To clean silver safely and quickly, line the bottom of a large plastic dish with doubled aluminum foil. Arrange the pieces of silver on it so that they don't touch each other. Pour on boiling water to which you have added 1 tablespoon of baking soda per quart. This works in a few minutes. Dry the pieces promptly. This method will even clean silver that is completely black.

—ROGER JOHNSON OF KENTVILLE, NOVA SCOTIA

Betty Revoy's Hummus

1 19-oz. can	chick peas, drain and reserve liquid	1 540-mL can
2	cloves garlic	2
3 heaping Tbsp.	tahini (sesame paste)	45 mL
1	lemon, juiced	1
2 tsp.	cumin	10 mL
1 tsp.	Nile spice (optional)	5 mL
	Pepper to taste	
1/3 cup	olive oil	75 mL
	Salt to taste	
	Garnish of olive oil, cayenne pepper, cumin, Greek olives, chopped parsley	

1 Fit food processor with a metal blade. Process drained chick peas and garlic until puréed. If the mixture is very thick, add a little of the reserved chick pea liquid.

2 Add tahini, lemon juice, cumin, Nile spice and pepper. Process again for a couple of minutes, using on/off motions, until thoroughly blended.

3 Add olive oil in a stream and process until mixture looks like a very thick mayonnaise. Taste and add salt if desired.

4 Spread mixture in a shallow bowl and drizzle with extra olive oil (do not flood the mixture). Sprinkle cayenne and cumin on top and decorate with olives and parsley. Serve with warmed pita bread triangles or savoury crackers.

C an it be true that we've finally given up on the garlic-dill-herb-baconette sort of sour cream chip dip! Abandoned the practice of grinding soup mix into a block of cream cheese! Hallelujah! Hummus may have saved us. It's true you can buy hummus in almost all stores now, but it's so much better when you control the combination of ingredients. Frankly, I would never have thought to make it myself until I met Betty Revoy, who knows plenty about Middle Eastern food preparation.

Born in Alexandria, Egypt, of Greek parents, Betty and her family moved to Montreal shortly before King Farouk went to live in permanent exile. Betty's mother and grandmother, both legendary cooks, taught her well. It used to be that cooks would bring into the studio—which is the size of a postage stamp—food already prepared. But now, unless we require an oven, we just invite people to slop the ingredients all over the studio.

Betty and I were very tidy, but the fabric walls of the closet/studio are now permeated with garlic. I try to keep this from the head of engineering at CBC.

Theresa's Fire Cookies

The day that Aldo Intrieri came into the studio was the day the world changed on my show. We'd finally figured out how to get free food—make the cookbook authors bring samples. Mr. Intrieri brought it in pails. We loved him. We think of him still. We want him to come back now. Theresa's Fire Cookies were a huge hit, and I've made the cabbage salad a lot. Mr. Intrieri is the owner of Aldo's Primavera Catering in Vancouver as well as the author of Break Loose—Spiced 'n' Spirited Cooking.

1/2 cup	butter	125 mL
1/4 tsp.	red pepper sauce	2 mL
1/4 tsp.	cayenne pepper	2 mL
1 cup	wholewheat flour	250 mL
1 cup	grated cheddar cheese	250 mL
1 cup	rice crispies	250 mL
2 Tbsp.	water	30 mL
	Salt to taste	

1 Preheat oven to 350°F (180°C).

2 In a medium bowl, mix butter, pepper sauce, cayenne pepper. Add remaining ingredients and mix well.

3 Roll dough into balls 1 inch (2.5 cm) in diameter and placed on a greased cookie sheet. Flatten with a fork. Bake for 15 to 20 minutes.

Makes 15 to 20 cookies.

Cabbage Salad

Dressing:

1/2 cup	olive oil	125 mL
1/2 tsp.	salt	3 mL
1 tsp.	pepper	5 mL
1 tsp.	sugar	5 mL
1	vegetable stock cube, crumbled	1
1/2 tsp.	basil	3 mL
1/2 tsp.	marjoram	3 mL

Salad:

1	small cabbage, shredded	1
2	green onions, sliced	2
2	red peppers, diced	2
1 pkg.	instant soup noodles, crumbled	1 pkg.
1 1/2 cups	toasted slivered almonds	375 mL
2 Tbsp.	toasted sesame seeds	30 mL

1 To make dressing: In a jar, add all the dressing ingredients and shake well.

2 To make salad: In a medium bowl, mix all the salad ingredients. Pour dressing over salad and refrigerate for several hours before serving.

Pete's Apple and Papaya Pick-Me-Up

P ete Luckett opened his first fruit and vegetable stand in Canada in the Saint John City Market in New Brunswick. It's a busy place, but even amidst the din you can hear Pete from a block away. Ebullient is the word for Pete. He spun into the studio with a recipe for a pick-me-up. Just what he needs.

He's also the co-author with Kathleen Robinson of Pete Luckett's Complete Guide to Fresh Fruit and Vegetables.

3	apples (your favourite local ones)	3
1	lime (or lemon, but lime is better)	1
1	ripe papaya (should be a rich yellow)	1
1/2	red onion, sliced very thin	1/2
1/2 cup	cottage cheese	125 mL
1 Tbsp.	chopped fresh herbs (recommend mint)	15 mL
1 Tbsp.	honey	15 mL
1/2 cup	oil and vinegar vinaigrette	125 mL

1 Peel, core and cut the 3 apples into wedges. Immediately sprinkle generously with lime juice.

2 Cut the ripe papaya in half, scoop out seeds and peel. Cut into thin slices and sprinkle with lime juice.

3 Arrange the apple and papaya on a plate with red onion slices and cottage cheese. Dissolve the honey in the vinaigrette and drizzle all over.

Rice-Ricotta Pancakes

A crepelike pancake with delicate texture and flavour—
delicious. This batter can be made either in a food processor or with an electric mixer. For a thicker pancake,
reduce the milk to 1/2 cup.

2	eggs	2
1/2 cup	ricotta cheese	125 mL
1 Tbsp.	vegetable oil	15 mL
1/2 cup	rice flour	125 mL
2 tsp.	sugar	10 mL
1 tsp.	baking powder	5 mL
1/2 tsp.	salt	2 mL
3/4 cup	milk (or nondairy liquid)	175 mL

1 Beat together the eggs and ricotta cheese and add the oil.

2 In a large measuring cup, mix flour, sugar, baking powder and salt. Beat into egg mixture alternately with the
milk. The mixture will be thin.

3 Pour onto either lightly greased or Teflon griddle and
bake at medium high. (Too hot a griddle will burn the
pancakes.)

Makes 1 dozen 4-inch (10-cm) pancakes.

*If you're allergic to wheat or rye flour, life can be diffi-
cult. Think about it. I never realized how many people had this
inability to digest gluten until Bette Hagman, a celiac herself, came on the show to talk about gluten-free cooking. We had
at least a thousand requests for more information and her
recipe for pancakes.*

*Gluten-free flour should be available in your health food store.
Also, Kay Spicer of Full of Beans fame intro-
duced a bean flour to me which is gluten-free.*

Bread and Butter Pudding

A bout a hundred years ago when I still lived at home with my parents, there took place a ritual that my addled teen brain couldn't grasp. My mother and father actually watched a guy on TV chop up stuff, fling great pieces of meat into a pan, swig back large glasses of wine and generally whirl around a kitchen set. On occasion, they would attempt to re-create the dish that had been so miraculously prepared by the goofy guy on TV. Sometimes it even worked.

Between then and now, that goofy guy on TV has undergone a tremendous transformation. Still the galloping gourmet, but no more wine swigging and precious little fat, he's written Graham Kerr's Smart Cooking. From it, here's his bread and butter pudding (except that there ain't no butter in it).

Bread and butter pudding is a British standard and many farms have family recipes. Because of the lush pastures and temperate climate, you get "cows upon cows." So it isn't surprising that buttered homemade bread is drowned in cream and eggs. I've tried hard to keep the "feelings" alive but reduce the fat. See what you think for yourself!

The big problem with desserts is that we insist upon whipped toppings, cream or ice cream as garnish. This simply increases the fat problem (and our waistline) and sometimes covers the essential flavours and textures of an otherwise great idea. My suggestion is to leave it alone. Let it be. The custard gives it built-in moisture.

8 Tbsp.	raisins	120 mL
1/4 cup	wheat germ	50 mL
2	large eggs	2
2 Tbsp.	brown sugar	30 mL
	Grated rind of 1 lemon	
2 cups	2 per cent milk	500 mL
4	slices wholewheat bread	4
4	slices white bread	4
1	whole cinnamon stick, about 1 1/2 inches/4 cm (or 1/2 tsp./2 mL grated)	1

1   Wash the raisins and then toss with the wheat germ. Sprinkle half this mixture evenly into a shallow, 3-cup (750-mL) capacity, ovenproof baking or pie dish.

2   Make an egg custard: Beat the eggs, 1 tablespoon (15 mL) of the brown sugar, milk and lemon rind together.

3   (With apologies to my homeland.) Leave the crust on the bread and cut it in half diagonally.

4   Arrange the bread slices in the baking dish so that they overlap. Press down to mould into the dish and then carefully pour the egg custard so that it soaks into the bread.

5   Grate the whole cinnamon and sprinkle it over the top. I use a small coffee mill to finely powder a cinnamon stick. Finally, sprinkle with the remaining raisins and brown sugar.

6   Place the baking pan in a bain-marie (another baking dish half-filled with water) and bake uncovered in a 350°F (180°C) oven for 30 to 35 minutes or until set. Serve warm.

Serves 6.

HOUSEHOLD HINTS
To clean a burnt pot, first let the pot dry. Pour vinegar into the pot so that it covers the bottom and let stand overnight. The burnt remains will scrape off with ease.

—LISA J. IZSO
OF CALGARY, ALBERTA

Flapper Pie

It may seem hard to believe, but I had never heard of or even seen this pie until the mid-seventies, when a girlfriend (who lifted the recipe right off the back of the graham wafer box) brought it over. I wept with pleasure. Carol Ferguson and her co-author Margaret Fraser included it in the 1920s chapter of their cookbook, A Century of Canadian Home Cooking. It doesn't look or taste like a contemporary dessert, and maybe that's what we all love about it.

In eastern Canada, this recipe was usually called Graham Wafer Cream Pie, but westerners knew it as Flapper Pie.

Crust:

1 1/4 cups	graham wafer crumbs	300 mL
1/4 cup	granulated sugar	50 mL
1/2 tsp.	cinnamon	2 mL
1/4 cup	butter, melted	50 mL

Filling:

1/4 cup	granulated sugar	50 mL
3 Tbsp.	cornstarch	50 mL
2 cups	milk	500 mL
2	egg yolks, lightly beaten	2
1 tsp.	vanilla	5 mL

Meringue:

2	egg whites	2
1/4 tsp.	cream of tartar	1 mL
2 Tbsp.	granulated sugar	25 mL

1 Crust: Combine crumbs, sugar and cinnamon; blend in butter. Set 1/4 cup (50 mL) aside. Press remainder onto bottom and sides of 9-inch (23-cm) pie plate. Bake in 375°F (190°C) oven for 8 minutes. Cool.

2 Filling: In saucepan, mix sugar with cornstarch; blend in milk. Cook over medium heat, stirring, until boiling; stir a little into yolks, then return to saucepan. Cook over low heat, stirring, for 2 minutes or until thickened. Remove from heat; add vanilla and cool slightly. Pour into pie crust.

3 Meringue: Beat egg whites with cream of tartar until soft peaks form; gradually beat in sugar until stiff peaks form. Spread over filling, sealing to crust. Top with reserved crumbs. Bake in 400°F (200°C) oven for 5 minutes or until lightly browned. Cool to room temperature, about 4 hours.

Variations

Banana Cream Pie: Into baked pie shell, slice 2 bananas. Pour Flapper Pie filling over top. Top with meringue or whipped cream.

Coconut Cream Pie: Add 1 cup (250 mL) shredded coconut to Flapper Pie filling. Pour into baked pie shell. Top with meringue or whipped cream.

Peanut Butter Beer Bread

When he was a food writer, Gordon was on the show a couple of times with great recipes. But the reason he will go down in the show's archives is that he is the only person we ever met who has actually taught courses about peanut butter.

He is now the book editor at the Edmonton Journal.

1/4 cup	butter, melted	50 mL
1/2 cup	crunchy peanut butter	125 mL
2 1/2 cups	all-purpose flour	625 mL
2 Tbsp.	sugar	25 mL
5 tsp.	baking powder	25 mL
1 tsp.	salt	5 mL
1 12-oz. bottle	beer	1 341-mL bottle

1. Preheat oven to 350°F (180°C).

2. In a large bowl, combine the butter and peanut butter.

3. In a medium bowl, combine the flour, sugar, baking powder and salt. Add dry mixture alternately with beer to the peanut butter mixture (making three dry and two liquid additions), combining well after each.

4. Pour into a greased 9 x 5-inch (23 x 13-cm) loaf pan and bake for 50 to 60 minutes or until loaf tests well done. Remove from pan and cool on a wire rack.

5. To serve, slice and toast. Spread with butter and jelly.

Makes 1 loaf.

Treacle or Molasses Scones

1	egg, beaten	1
4 Tbsp.	molasses	50 mL
1/2 cup	milk	125 mL
2	cups sifted flour	500 mL
1/2 tsp.	salt (optional)	2 mL
2 tsp.	baking powder	10 mL
1/4 tsp.	baking soda	1 mL
1 tsp.	nutmeg	5 mL
1 tsp.	cinnamon	5 mL
1 tsp.	ginger	5 mL
2/3 cup	brown sugar	150 mL
1/3 cup	margarine (or butter)	75 mL

1 Preheat oven to 400°F (200°C).

2 In a small bowl, mix together egg, molasses and milk. Set aside.

3 In a large bowl, mix together dry ingredients and cut in the margarine or butter. Add wet ingredients and mix to the consistency of biscuit dough.

4 Roll or pat dough to a 1/2 inch (1 cm) thickness and cut out the scones. Place scones on a lightly greased cookie sheet. Bake for 15 to 18 minutes.

Peanut Butter Cookies

D avid Wood, who used to own a fancy food store called David Wood Foods on Yonge Street in Toronto, and who produced several good cookbooks, sold his business and had the sense to move to the Gulf Islands.

Whereas David is known as a gourmet and an accomplished chef, we asked him to supply "something with peanut butter" when we invited him to play on the radio. A cookie, maybe! He might have preferred to represent himself in a more elaborate way, but the peanut butter cookie obsession, yet another of our of our cockamamie tangents, had a fevered grip on the program that could only be stilled by this recipe. There were hundreds of requests for this hit from The David Wood Food Book.

1 1/2 cups	all-purpose flour	375 mL
1/4 tsp.	baking soda	2 mL
5 oz.	butter	140 g
1/2 cup	granulated sugar	125 mL
1/2 cup	light brown sugar, firmly packed	125 mL
1 1/2 tsp.	vanilla	7 mL
1	egg	1
1/2 cup	smooth peanut butter	125 mL
3/4 cup	salted peanuts	175 mL

1 Preheat the oven to 375°F (190°C).

2 Sift together the flour and baking soda; set aside.

3 Cream the butter in an electric mixer (or with a hand mixer). Add both the sugars and the vanilla and cream until light and fluffy (1 to 2 minutes).

4 Beat in the egg; then reduce the mixer speed to low and add half the sifted flour. Stop the mixer and scrape down the sides of the bowl.

5 Add the peanut butter and beat until smooth. Scrape down the sides again. Add the rest of the flour and the peanuts and mix again. The dough may be quite stiff. Don't worry—knead it a little by hand to bring it together if necessary.

6 Scoop out the dough into roughly 1 1/2-oz. (40-g) balls (you can use an ice-cream scoop). Set them on an ungreased cookie sheet, and press down with the palm of your hand to flatten them to about 1/2 inch (1 cm) thick.

7 With the back of a fork, make a criss-cross pattern on top. Bake for about 12 minutes until they are very lightly browned. Watch them carefully; they burn quite easily.

Makes 48 cookies.

Variation

Chocolate Chunk Peanut Butter Cookies: Make the cookies as directed above. At step 7, just before putting them in the oven, press 2 or 3 chunks of chocolate into the top of each cookie. Bake as directed.

Orange-Pineapple Cream Ramen

A unique dessert that is quick and easy to make and tastes simply wonderful.

1 1/2 cups	orange juice	375 mL
1 pkg.	ramen noodles, crushed	1 pkg.
1/4 cup	whipped topping	50 mL
1/4 cup	sour cream	50 mL
1 5-oz. can	pineapple chunks, drained	1 142-mL can
1 11-oz. can	mandarin oranges, drained	1 312-mL can

1 Bring orange juice to boil. Crush noodles in package and add to orange juice, cover and cook over medium-low heat for 10 minutes. Remove from heat, set aside for 5 minutes and let noodles absorb all the liquid.

2 In a small bowl, mix together whipped topping and sour cream.

3 Put noodles in a larger bowl. Add topping mixture, pineapple and mandarin oranges and toss well. Can be eaten immediately or chilled.

R on Konzak lives in Friday Harbor, in Washington State, a two-hour drive and four-hour border wait away from Vancouver. He's not really a chef: he's more a musician, inventor and eccentric. Did I mention that he's a Buddhist who plays the Celtic harp! And he has written a cookbook centred on ramen, those dried and pressed squiggly Japanese noodles that you can buy at any store for almost no money. In fact, Ron claims you can feed your entire family for a week for less than five bucks ($7.95 Canadian).

This is as odd a dessert as you might think, but do give it a try. A word of advice: don't forget to omit the ramen flavour pack when you make it.

HOUSEHOLD HINTS

To collect cat and dog hair on chairs, couches, rugs, etc., put on a pair of rubber kitchen gloves and rub your hands along the surface. The hair will accumulate in a little ball, ready to throw away.

—STEPHANIE FOSTER OF BANCROFT, ONTARIO

Jamaican Ginger Beer— Northern Version

I include this ginger beer recipe as a nice accompaniment to your Venison Piquant (see the index for its whereabouts in this book). This ginger beer is referred to as the northern version. What the southern version would include, I can't imagine.

For the fresh ginger, plump Jamaican ginger is the best.

1	whole pineapple, peeled and cut up into bite-size pieces	1
2 oz.	fresh ginger, grated	55 g
1/2–1 cup	brown sugar, to taste	125–250 mL

1 In a saucepan, bring 5 cups (1.25 L) of water to a boil. Remove from heat. Add pineapple and ginger. Let steep for 8 hours. Add sugar to taste.

2 Strain, bottle and refrigerate.

3 If you want some bubbles, add sparkling mineral water when serving.

Ginger Ale

1	lemon wedge	1	
1/4-inch slice	ginger root	5-mm slice	
1	medium bunch green grapes	1	
	Sparkling water		

1 Juice lemon. Push ginger through hopper with grapes. Pour juice into tall, ice-filled glass. Fill glass to top with sparkling water.

N onalcoholic fruit and vegetable drinks are a welcome trend. I guess you don't really need a juicer— you could use a blender or a food processor, or you could beat the ingredients with a baseball bat—but the fact is that a juicer is a real boon.

Remember the days when anyone who drank carrot juice (for instance, Jack La Laine, the guy who in his eighth decade still manages to swim across San Francisco harbour pulling a boat with his teeth), was considered a nutter! Now, you're almost a nutter if you don't. Here are three recipes from Cherie Calbom and Maureen Keane, both American nutri- tionists, from their book Juicing for Life. Cherie Calbom is also co-author with Vickie Rae Chelf of Cooking for Life.

Garden Salad Special

3	broccoli flowerets	3
1	clove garlic	1
4 to 5	carrots (or 2 tomatoes)	4 to 5
2	stalks celery	2
1/2	green pepper	1/2

1 Push broccoli and garlic through hopper with carrots or tomatoes. Follow with celery and green pepper.

HOUSEHOLD HINTS

To scrub clean a large amount of fresh, dirty carrots, rinse off the worst of the dirt and then dump the lot into your washing machine. *Do not add soap!* Set washer to a medium-length cycle on warm, and then to rinse on cold, and the gentle cycle on spin dry. Lay the clean carrots out to dry for an hour or so, then store in a cool place in perforated bags.

—**LYNN KIRK**
OF REGINA, SASKATCHEWAN

Hair-Growth Cocktail

2	dark green lettuce leaves	2
	Handful alfalfa sprouts	
4 to 5	carrots, greens removed	4 to 5

1 Bunch up lettuce and alfalfa, and push through hopper with carrots.

Gold Strike

For those of you who still consume alcohol, this is allegedly a sure-fire hangover cure. It's from The Canadian Honey Recipe Book, published by the B.C. Honey Producer's Association.

1	egg	1
1 cup	chilled orange juice	250 mL
1 Tbsp.	honey	15 mL

1 Combine all ingredients; beat or blend until frothy. Serve at once, with warmed-up bran muffins.

Serves 1.

HOUSEHOLD HINTS

When hammering, if you miss the nail or pound it too hard and make a dent in the wood (called a cat's eye), put some water on it and it will return to normal in twenty-four hours.

—Tim Elmsley
OF MASSET, B.C.

2

Fancy and
Fabulous

Shrimp Dijonaise

2 Tbsp.	butter	30 mL
1 Tbsp.	minced shallots	15 mL
16	large shrimp, peeled and deveined	16
1/2 cup	flour	125 mL
3/8 cup	white wine	100 mL
2 tsp.	Dijon mustard	10 mL
	Pinch of chopped parsley	
	Few dashes bitters	
	Salt and pepper to taste	
1	lemon for garnish	1

1 In a sauté pan, heat butter over medium heat.

2 Add minced shallots and heat for approximately 30 seconds.

3 Dredge shrimp in flour and add to the pan. Cook shrimp for *approximately* 1 minute on each side. *Do not overcook.*

4 Deglaze the pan with white wine. Add Dijon mustard, chopped parsley, bitters, salt and pepper. Combine and let the wine reduce to a sauce.

5 When the sauce is slightly thickened, arrange the shrimp on the plates. Spoon sauce over the shrimp and garnish the plates with a lemon crown.

Serves 2.

H *ave I told you four or five times already that I work in a studio the size of a twin bed? Oh. Then you'll understand that when the large hunks of human flesh that are the Clever Cleaver brothers came bolting through the door with their frying pan and a mountain of shrimp, there was no space left to take a deep breath. These boys were not only big, they were energetic. They jumped up and down, they sang, they danced, they left an impression and some very good shrimp from their* Cookin' with the Cleavers.

Chez Bob's Caesar Salad

I *t's understand-able that professional chefs travel with their own equipment, but I've only met one guy who carries along his own salad bowl in a kit designed for a snare drum. He even takes it with him on the plane. Maybe it has its own seat, like Nigel Kennedy and his Stradivarius— Bob and his bowl. I guess you could call Bob a kitchen musician.*

In his cookbook The Surreal Gourmet: Real Food for Pretend Chefs, *he provides not only swell recipes but also musical accompaniments to round out your meal with style. He claims that this is a sure-fire, win-win combination, if you get my drift. He suggests that Leonard Cohen's "I'm Your Man" and his Caesar salad form the perfect combo. It works for me.*

The anchovy is, of course, optional. I find that the flavour of olive oil overwhelms the dressing so I use safflower oil. However, most back-seat chefs I know disagree. Mark Collins, a chef friend of mine from Toronto, eliminates the anchovy and adds a sun-dried tomato in oil which he blends into the paste.

Lettuce leaves should be coated but not soaked in dressing. Adjust amount of dressing for more or less lettuce to keep salad from becoming too "wet."

Use imported Italian Reggiano Parmesan, grated just before using (the key to the definitive Caesar) and good croutons. The best croutons are made from thickly sliced, slightly stale flavourful breads (e.g. sourdough, Italian and pumpernickel).

Croutons:

4 slices	bread, cut into 3/4-inch (2-cm) cubes	4 slices
1/3 cup	olive oil	75 mL
1	clove garlic, minced (optional)	1
1 tsp.	any dried herbs (oregano, thyme, basil—optional)	5 mL
1	medium to large head of romaine lettuce	1
1/2 tsp.	salt	2 mL
1 tsp.	coarse black pepper	5 mL
1 to 3	cloves garlic (depending on you and your guests' garlic threshold), minced	1 to 3
1	anchovy (or 1 tsp./5 mL anchovy paste—optional)	1
1 Tbsp.	Dijon mustard (the real stuff, not the dried stuff)	15 mL
1	egg yolk	1
	Juice of 1/2 lemon	
1 tsp.	Worcestershire sauce	5 mL
1 tsp.	red wine vinegar	5 mL
1/3 cup	vegetable (or olive) oil	75 mL
1/3 cup	grated Parmesan cheese	75 mL
1 cup	croutons	250 mL

1 To make the croutons: Place bread cubes in a large bowl, add oil and other ingredients. Toss until oil is absorbed. Place on a cookie sheet or tin foil and bake in a preheated oven at 350°F (180°C) for approximately 25 minutes until browned. Turn once or twice so that all sides brown evenly.

2 To assemble the salad: Discard outer leaves of lettuce. Wash and dry remaining leaves thoroughly, then slice into bite-size pieces.

3 Into a large wooden salad bowl, add ingredients up to the vinegar in order, one at a time. After adding each ingredient, use the back side of a soup spoon to blend it with the previous ingredients into a smooth paste.

4 Add vinegar and oil and blend well.

5 *Just* before serving, add lettuce and toss thoroughly.

6 Add cheese and croutons, toss again and serve.

Serves 2 as a meal, 4 as a salad course.

Stand-up Sesame Caesar Salad

Yet another twist on the Caesar salad, this time from Kasey Wilson, who can come on my show anytime she wants. She talks and talks and talks (which is good on radio). Besides, she really knows how to cook and is an inspired chef. Her more recent cookbooks are Gifts from the Kitchen *and* Spirit and Style.

This recipe of hers not only tastes great but has a spectacular presentation that will make you appear to be a highly skilled chef yourself (unless you drop it on the floor or something).

1	head romaine lettuce	

Croutons:

1/2 cup	olive oil	125 mL
1 tsp.	Asian (toasted) sesame oil	5 mL
1 loaf	french bread, cut into 4 x 1/2-inch (10 x 1-cm) slices	1 loaf
1/4 cup	chopped fresh cilantro (coriander)	50 mL

Sesame dressing:

1/4 cup	fresh lemon juice	50 mL
2	egg yolks	2
1	anchovy fillet, minced (optional)	1
1/4 tsp.	Tabasco sauce	1 mL
2	garlic cloves, minced	2
2 Tbsp.	Dijon mustard	25 mL
3–5 Tbsp.	sour cream	45–75 mL
1 cup plus 3 Tbsp.	olive oil	300 mL
3 Tbsp.	freshly grated Parmesan cheese	45 mL
1/4 cup	sesame seeds, toasted	50 mL
	Salt and freshly ground pepper to taste	
2	tomatoes in 1/2-inch (1-cm) cubes (or sun-dried tomato strips)	2

1 Wash the whole lettuce leaves, dry thoroughly and refrigerate.

2 To make the croutons: Add the olive oil and sesame oil to a skillet over moderate heat. Add the bread strips and cilantro and stir for several minutes, or until the bread is crisp and golden. Spread on paper towels to cool.

3 To make the sesame dressing: In a blender or food processor, place lemon juice, egg yolks, anchovy, Tabasco, garlic, mustard and sour cream; process until smooth. With the machine running, slowly add the oil in a thin, steady stream. It will thicken like whipping cream. Add the Parmesan cheese. (If you're using a blender, you may have to prepare the dressing in 2 batches.) Add sesame seeds, salt and pepper.

4 To assemble the salad: Lay out the whole romaine leaves on a countertop. Spread each leaf with sesame dressing along the middle. Add one or two croutons to the centre. Add tomato cubes or sun-dried tomato strips. Wrap the lettuce leaf around the filling and place "taco-like" on a platter to pass around as hors d'oeuvres.

Gazpacho Andalucia (Spanish Cold Soup)

John Bishop is the proprietor of one great restaurant, curiously named Bishop's. It is very famous, not just for the consistently high quality of its cuisine but also for the extreme charm of Mr. Bishop and his well chosen comical staff. And movie stars go there! I saw Robert De Niro, Sean Penn and our own Jack Webster there all in one evening. It ain't cheap, but they're not grinders of widows and orphans either. Mr. Bishop has visited my studio twice and left behind two recipes for free.

1 1/2 lb.	tomatoes, cut into quarters	700 g
8 oz.	cucumber, cut into 1/2-inch (1-cm) cubes	250 g
7 oz.	green pimentos, seeded, in 1/4-inch (5-mm) cubes	200 g
6	small cloves garlic, peeled and crushed	6
2/3 cup	olive oil	150 mL
1/2 oz.	cumin seed, crushed	15 g
2 1/2 cups or more	tomato juice	600 mL or more
3/8 cup	vinegar	100 mL

Salt and pepper to taste
Ice to chill mixture
Garnish of small croutons, finely diced green pepper, finely diced onion, finely diced cucumber, finely diced blanched tomatoes

1 In a blender, combine tomatoes, cucumber, pimentos, garlic, olive oil, cumin, tomato juice and vinegar. Blend. Check seasoning and consistency. Pour into a bain-marie container. Chill on ice, store in refrigerator.

2 Garnish soup just before serving.

Serves 12 to 14.

Crabcakes with Roasted Red Pepper Mayonnaise

To reduce the cost, substitute hand-peeled shrimp for half the crab. In summer, instead of the red pepper mayonnaise, serve the crabcakes with a salsa of fresh strawberries, red onions and lime juice that has ripened for at least half an hour. Garnish with fresh fruit sage and pineapple sage.

Red pepper mayonnaise:

1	red bell pepper	1
	Vegetable oil	
1 cup	mayonnaise	250 mL

Crabcakes:

1 lb.	fresh crabmeat	500 g
1 1/2 cups	fresh bread crumbs	375 mL
1 cup	mayonnaise	250 mL
2 Tbsp.	red bell peppers, chopped	30 mL
10	large basil leaves, coarsely chopped	10
1	green onion, chopped	1
	Salt and pepper	
	Flour for dredging	
1 Tbsp.	vegetable oil	15 mL

1 Preheat oven to 450°F (230°C).

2 To prepare the red pepper mayonnaise: Place red pepper on baking sheet and lightly brush with oil. Bake for 15 minutes or until slightly charred. Remove and place in a brown paper bag to cool. Peel off the skin from the pepper, halve and remove seeds. In a food processor, purée the pepper with the mayonnaise.

3 To prepare the crabcakes: In a large bowl, combine the crab, bread crumbs, mayonnaise, red pepper, basil, onion, salt and pepper to taste. Shape into 8 balls. Lightly dredge in flour, shaking off the excess.

4 In a cast-iron skillet, heat the oil over medium heat. Place crabcake balls in pan and lightly press with the back of a spatula to flatten to 3/4 inch (2 cm) thickness. Be gentle with the crabcakes—they are fragile. Fry for three minutes per side or until golden brown.

Serves 4.

The Gazpacho Andalucia is divine, and the crabcakes will end your search for the perfect crabcake. I can die a happy woman now. The crabcakes are touchy items to prepare because they might fall apart, but if you are gentle and don't rush, you will have your friends and family begging for more. Begging is good.

Smoked Salmon Cardamom Spread

W hy is it that we hang onto expressions like "you know," "you bet" and "that's fer sure"? Probably because they're spacers and give us time to think. I need all the time I can get to think, so I have a stack of these spacers. Some of them the crew has asked me to remove from my vocabulary, mostly because they're sick of hearing them. Fine!

One of my worst or most often used expressions is, "Can I come over?" I say it to an alarming number of people: lords of manors, scientists in the field, and especially owners of exquisite and remote fishing resorts in Alaska. Here's a favourite from The Riversong Lodge Cookbook.

Smoked salmon, sour cream and cardamom is a flavour blend I discovered one day by accident. We chill champagne in the snow to serve with this spread for a special winter appetizer.

Other flavourings, such as fresh chopped basil, cayenne pepper or sun-dried tomatoes, can be substituted for the cardamom.

1 lb.	kippered salmon	500 g
3/4 cup	sour cream	175 mL
1/2 tsp.	ground cardamom	2 mL
	Freshly ground pepper to taste	
1	lemon	1

1 Chop half of the kippered salmon in the bowl of a food processor. Add the sour cream, cardamom and pepper. Grate the zest of the lemon into the salmon mixture. Squeeze one-half of the lemon's juices into the mixture as well. Process the salmon mixture until it is puréed. Transfer the purée to a large bowl.

2 Coarsely chop the remaining salmon and add it to the purée. Mix well, cover and refrigerate until serving time.

3 Serve a dollop of spread on favourite crackers or bread.

Makes 1 1/2 lb. (750 g) or 24 1-oz. (30-g) servings.

Eastern Graphic Shellfish Stew Puissant

This recipe was put together when I was doing a lot of freelance work for the *Graphic*, hence the title. The word "puissant" has several connotations, mostly having to do with being powerful.

Use fresh garden or hothouse tomatoes, not the bricks usually sold in stores. Two bottles of wine are needed—one cup for the stew and the rest for the cooks to drink while cooking.

4 Tbsp	olive oil	60 mL
1	large onion, chopped	1
2	large cloves garlic, minced	2
2	celery stalks, including leaves, chopped	2
1	carrot, chopped	1
4 lb.	tomatoes, chopped	1.8 kg
2 Tbsp.	tomato paste	30 mL
1 cup	or more dry white wine	250 mL
1 lb.	scallops, cut in half	500 g
1 dozen	mussels	1 dozen
1 dozen	small quahogs	1 dozen
1 can	baby clams	1 can
1 11.3-oz. can	crab meat	1 320-g can
2 11.3-oz. cans	lobster meat	2 320-g cans
1 sm can	whole shrimp	1 sm can
	Pinch saffron	
	Salt and pepper	
	Garnish of fresh parsley, finely chopped	

1 In a large heavy cook pot, heat olive oil and gently sauté onion and garlic until transparent. Add celery, carrot, tomatoes, tomato paste, 1 cup (250 mL) of water and stir. Cover and simmer gently for 15 minutes.

2 Add the wine, scallops, mussels and quahogs, stirring well. Cover and simmer for 10 minutes. Add the clams, crab, lobster, shrimp, saffron, salt and pepper. If the stew appears to be too thick, add some more wine or water. Cook for 5 to 6 minutes more.

3 Discard any shellfish that have not opened. Sprinkle with parsley and serve.

John Gracey is the editor of Atlantic Farming Magazine *in Prince Edward Island. He is also an extravagant cook in that he seems to care not a whit that this dish costs about the same as the gross national product of Suriname. More, maybe.*

This seafood stew was entered in the Prince Edward Island Department of Fisheries cooking contest. It is reported that it came second only because no one in her right mind would fork out the dough required to produce it. So sell a bond and wow your friends.

Mr. Gracey and I prepared this dish in the kitchen of long-suffering CBC Charlottetown freelancer Kim Devine. Halfway through, her dentist husband, Don, barged in and wanted to know what was for lunch. He got this, and later we made him wear an Anne of Green Gables red-yarn wig.

Pear Upside-Down Gingerbread

I first met Eve Johnson in the early 1980s in New York City at one of the world's craziest restaurants, Sammy's Romanian Steak House. They serve red wine by the pail and they have seltzer bottles on the tables, with a warning that if you squirt anybody, you're out of there. Things must have got out of hand in the past. Ours was such a wild evening that when Mort Freeman, the entertainment, got up and sang "My Yiddishe Momma," some of us—okay, most of us—burst into tears.

Gingerbread is a homey affair, simple to make and endlessly satisfying. This dramatic version, which joins pears and ginger in a particularly inspired union, is best served warm with whipped cream.

3	pears, peeled and halved	3
1 1/4 cups	all-purpose flour	300 mL
3/4 tsp.	baking soda	4 mL
1 tsp.	ground cinnamon	5 mL
1/2 tsp.	ground ginger	2 mL
1/4 tsp.	ground cloves	1 mL
1/2 tsp.	salt	2 mL
1/2 cup	buttermilk	125 mL
1/4 cup	soft shortening	50 mL
1/4 cup	sugar	50 mL
1	large egg	1
1/2 cup	table molasses	125 mL
1/4 cup	chopped nuts	50 mL
	Whipped cream (or ice cream) for topping	

1 Place pear halves, cut-side down and stem end toward centre, in well-greased 9-inch (23-cm) round cake pan; set aside.

2 In large bowl, combine flour, baking soda, cinnamon, ginger, cloves and salt.

3 In blender or food processor, blend buttermilk, shortening, sugar, egg and molasses until smooth, about 2 minutes. Pour over dry ingredients and mix thoroughly.

4 Pour batter over pears and sprinkle with nuts. Bake at 350°F (180°C) for 40 to 45 minutes. Loosen cake from edges of pan and invert immediately onto serving plate. Serve warm, topped with whipped cream.

Serves 6.

Roasted Carrot and Brie Soup

Roasted carrots are as sweet as candy. Combine them with brie and whipping cream, and you have a luxurious winter soup. We found it on the menu at the Chateau Whistler Resort and asked executive chef Bernard Casavant for the recipe.

2 Tbsp.	butter (or margarine)	30 mL
3 cups	coarsely chopped carrots	750 mL
1/2 cup	coarsely chopped Spanish onions	125 mL
6 cups	chicken stock	1.5 L
	Salt and freshly ground pepper to taste	
3 oz.	brie cheese, rind removed	75 g
3/4 cup	whipping cream	175 mL

1 Melt butter in 9-inch (23-cm) square baking pan in 450°F (230°C) oven. Add carrots and roast for 20 minutes or until lightly browned, stirring occasionally.

2 Transfer carrots and butter to large heavy saucepan. Add onions and cook until onions are translucent, about 3 to 5 minutes. Add chicken stock. Season with salt and pepper and simmer for 30 minutes or until carrots are soft.

3 Pour about one-third of the soup into blender. Cut cheese into small pieces and add to soup in blender; blend until smooth. Pour into a clean saucepan. Blend remaining soup and add to saucepan. Add cream and correct seasonings if necessary.

Serves 6.

The next time Eve and I met, it was slightly less woolly, but not without madness. She brought in a recipe for Roasted Carrot and Brie Soup, which she proceeded to prepare. It took two hours to cook the carrots on our modest hot plate. Such are the test kitchen facilities at the CBC, unlike those at the Vancouver Sun. *Here is the meal she made for me that day: Roasted Carrot and Brie Soup, Onion Bread (made with Quick Pizza Dough) and Pear Upside-Down Gingerbread from her Five Star Cookbook.*

Quick Pizza Dough

The quick pizza dough makes a fine pizza, but you can also use it as a springboard for a multitude of easy breads. My favourite deviation is to sauté an onion in a little oil very gently while the dough rises, then spread the sautéed onion over the dough and sprinkle it with black, onion-fragrant kalonji seeds (often used in Bengali cooking and available at spice stores and ethnic markets) before I put it in the oven. The double onion flavour is wonderfully rich.

This bread, adapted from a recipe in *Eating Well* magazine, has been part of my kitchen ever since I tested it. If you let the food processor do the kneading, it's unbelievably fast.

This recipe makes enough pizza dough to serve 4. If there are only 2 of you, make the whole recipe, let the dough rest 10 minutes after kneading, then punch it down and cut it in two. Put half in a plastic bag and refrigerate it. The dough will keep 24 hours in the fridge. An hour before you want supper, take the dough out of its plastic bag and let it come to room temperature before baking.

4–4 1/2 cups	all-purpose flour	1–1.125 L
2 8-g pkg.	instant yeast	2 8-g pkg.
2 tsp.	salt	10 mL
1 tsp.	sugar	5 mL
	Water	
2 tsp.	olive oil	10 mL
	Cornmeal	

Food processor method:

1 In a large-capacity food processor fitted with a steel blade, combine 4 cups (1 L) of the flour, yeast, salt and sugar.

2 Heat 1 1/2 cups (375 mL) water and olive oil until very warm, 125°F to 130°F (50°C to 55°C). With the motor running, gradually pour the warm water mixture through the feed tube. Process, adding up to 2 tablespoons (30 mL) cold water until the dough forms a ball, then process for one minute to knead.

3 Turn dough out onto lightly floured surface, cover with plastic wrap and let rest for 10 minutes.

Conventional method:

1 In a large bowl, combine 3 cups (750 mL) of flour, yeast, salt and sugar.

2 Heat 1 3/4 cups (425 mL) water and olive oil until very warm, 125°F to 130°F (50°C to 55°C).

3 With a wooden spoon, gradually stir the warm water mixture into the flour mixture; beat well until mixed. Gradually add enough of the remaining flour to make a soft but not sticky dough.

4 Turn dough out onto a lightly floured surface and knead for 8 to 10 minutes or until smooth and elastic, adding flour if needed. Cover with plastic wrap and let rest for 10 minutes.

To make pizza:

1 Place an inverted large baking sheet on the lowest rack of the oven. Preheat oven to 500°F (260°C).

2 Divide pizza dough into eight pieces. Using your fists, stretch one piece into a 6-inch (15-cm) round. (Or roll out on a lightly floured surface with a rolling pin.) Keep remaining dough covered with a towel or plastic wrap as you work.

3 Dust another inverted baking sheet with cornmeal. Place the pizza round on it. Stretch or roll a second round and place beside the first. Top as desired.

4 Carefully slide the pizzas onto the hot inverted baking sheet in oven. Bake for 10 to 14 minutes or until the bottoms are crisp and browned. Working with two pizzas at a time, repeat with the remaining dough.

Makes eight 6-inch (15-cm) pizzas.

HOUSEHOLD HINTS

To clean the inside of a stained dishwasher, dump one package of Tang orange crystals into the dishwasher. Put it through a regular cycle (no soap). It will be sparkling clean!

—CAROL MCGEAUGHLIN OF THORNHILL, ONTARIO

The Great Vegetarian Unturkey

One of the hard things about becoming a vegetarian is the family ceremony dinner, when others want to eat the traditional turkey or ham or whatever. You don't want to eat flesh, but you don't want to miss out on the celebration, either. So Vesanto Melina and Joseph Forrest, who is a professional chef and caterer, came up with the "unturkey." Ms. Melina is a registered dietitian specializing in vegetarian nutrition and a vegetarian cookbook author (co-author with Brenda Davis and Victoria Harrison of Becoming Vegetarian). She says this recipe is based on one developed by Martha Rose Shulman in Fast Vegetarian Feasts. What's great about this dish is that it also looks festive and smells great. And it's got gravy too.

Unturkey (squash):

1 5-lb.	autumn squash (buttercup, corn, red curry, etc.)	1 2.5-kg

Lentils for stuffing:

1/2 cup	lentils	125 mL
2 cups	water	500 mL
1/8 tsp.	thyme	0.5 mL
1	bay leaf	1
1/2	small onion, chopped and sautéed	1/2
1/2	clove garlic	1/2
	Pinch of salt	
1/2 cup	rice	125 mL
1/2 cup	millet	125 mL

Stuffing:

1 Tbsp.	vegetable oil	15 mL
1	small onion, chopped	1
1	clove garlic, minced	1
1 1/2 cups	lentils, cooked	375 mL
1 cup	brown rice, cooked	250 mL
1 cup	millet, cooked	250 mL
1/2 cup	almonds (or cashews or pecans), chopped	125 mL
2 Tbsp.	sunflower seeds	30 mL
1/4 cup	stoneground yellow cornmeal	50 mL
1	rib celery, chopped	1
1 cup	broccoli florets, steamed briefly until bright green	250 mL
1 tsp.	dried leaf sage	5 mL
1 tsp.	ground celery seed	5 mL
2 tsp.	tamari (or soy sauce)	10 mL
1/2 cup	wholewheat bread crumbs	125 mL
	Salt and pepper to taste	

Gravy:

3 Tbsp.	vegetable oil	45 mL
2 Tbsp.	onion, finely chopped	30 mL
1 tsp.	garlic, minced	5 mL
1/4 tsp.	dried rosemary	1 mL
3 Tbsp.	flour	45 mL
2 cups	vegetable stock, made from vegetable bouillon cubes	500 mL
	Salt and pepper to taste	

1 To prepare the squash: Set the squash on a rack in a roasting pan and steam for 30 minutes. Rinse the squash in cold water. With a sharp knife, cut and remove a circular piece from the top of the squash—the hole should be large enough to accommodate your hand or a large spoon. Through the hole, scoop out seeds and pulp. Brush the insides with oil or melted butter.

2 To prepare the lentils for the stuffing: Put all the ingredients in a covered saucepan and bring to a boil. Lower heat and simmer for 1 hour. Drain, but reserve the cooking liquid.

3 To prepare the brown rice : Bring 1/2 cup (125 mL) of brown rice and 1 cup (250 mL) of water to boil in a covered saucepan. Lower heat and simmer for 45 minutes.

4 To prepare the millet : Bring 1/2 cup (125 mL) of millet and 1 cup (250 mL) of water to boil in a covered saucepan. Lower heat and simmer for 20 minutes.

5 Preheat oven to 350°F (180°C).

6 Stuffing: In a skillet, heat the oil and sauté onions and garlic until soft.

7 In a large bowl, combine all the stuffing ingredients. If the stuffing is too stiff, add some of the liquid from the cooked lentils. If the stuffing is not stiff enough, add more bread crumbs.

8 Stuff the squash with as much stuffing as you can squeeze inside. Put leftover stuffing into an oiled loaf pan. Replace the squash lid. Set squash upright in an oiled roasting pan. Bake for 1 hour or until a toothpick can be inserted easily. Remove from the oven.

9 To make the gravy: In a medium-size saucepan, heat oil and sauté onion, garlic and rosemary until soft. Add flour to make a roux and cook, stirring constantly, for a few minutes until it just begins to brown. Slowly pour in the stock, stirring all the while until it thickens, about 10 minutes. Add salt and pepper to taste.

Serves 10 to 12.

N athan Hyam used to be a social worker with a particular interest in youths who had temporarily lost their way. But youths must eat. So Nathan and a friend, David Dranchuk, had the advanced idea of combining the need to eat, to work and to find their way in the form of a restaurant. The Picasso restaurant in Vancouver still thrives, continuing to train young people for the food industry.

Mr. Hyam has moved on. Now he teaches grown-up people how to cook, even matrons like me. When I went to visit him at the Cook School at the Cook Shop in Vancouver, he had designed not just a couple of recipes but an entire Thai dinner. I include it all here so that you can prepare a feast for your friends and family. Good luck.

NOTE: The meal that Nathan prepared was modestly hot, but I like rocket fuel, so I would double the hot sauce on every occasion—don't be a baby.

Chicken Satay with Peanut Sauce

Thai coconut marinade for satay:

1 14-oz. can	coconut milk	1 398-mL can
3	cloves garlic, minced	3
1/4 cup	cilantro, chopped	50 mL
1 tsp.	fresh ginger, minced	5 mL
1 Tbsp.	soy sauce	15 mL
1 tsp.	hot sauce	5 mL

Strips of chicken (or beef or pork)

Peanut sauce:

	Vegetable oil	
1/4 cup	onion, diced	50 mL
1 1/2 Tbsp.	fresh ginger, minced	25 mL
1	clove garlic, minced	1
1/2 cup	chunky peanut butter	125 mL
3/4 cup	coconut milk	175 mL
1 tsp.	hot sauce	5 mL
1 1/2 Tbsp.	brown sugar	25 mL
2 Tbsp.	soy sauce	30 mL
1/4 cup	cilantro leaves, sliced	50 mL

1 Marinade: In a large bowl, whisk together coconut milk, garlic, cilantro, ginger, soy sauce and hot sauce. Marinate chicken for 6 hours or overnight in refrigerator.

2 Thread meat onto skewers and grill, or drain meat and bake in a hot oven.

3 Peanut sauce: In a frying pan, heat some oil and sauté the onion, ginger and garlic until soft, about one minute. Add all the other ingredients except the cilantro and simmer on low heat until the peanut butter is melted, about 5 minutes. Add cilantro and set aside. Serve with the chicken satay.

Cucumber Pickles

1 1/2 cups	Japanese (or English) cucumbers, sliced thin	375 mL
1/4 cup	coarsely chopped shallots (or red onion)	50 mL
1 or 2	red Thai chilies, seeded and finely chopped	1 or 2
1 Tbsp.	cilantro, chopped	15 mL
1/4 cup	rice vinegar	50 mL
1 tsp.	brown sugar	5 mL
1/8 tsp.	salt (optional)	0.5 mL
1/4 cup	roasted peanuts, chopped (optional)	50 mL

1 Combine all the ingredients and serve as a side dish with the satay.

Chicken and Peppers in a Red Coconut Curry

Thai red coconut curry paste:

7 to 10	medium-size dried hot red peppers	7 to 10
2-inch cube	fresh galanga root (or 2 tsp./10 mL powdered)	5-cm cube
1	stalk fresh lemongrass (or 3 tsp./15 mL dried pieces)	1
3	garlic cloves	3
6	shallots	6
4 to 5	fresh cilantro roots (about 10 stems)	4 to 5
2 tsp.	paprika	10 mL
1/2 tsp.	ground coriander	2 mL
1/2 tsp.	ground cumin seeds	2 mL
1/4 tsp.	turmeric	1 mL
Pinch	cinnamon	Pinch
2 to 3 1/2-inch	pieces lime rind, finely chopped	2 to 3 1-cm
1 1/2 tsp.	shrimp paste	7 mL
Pinch	salt	Pinch
1/2	red bell pepper, diced	1/2

1 Remove and discard the seeds from the dried hot peppers and place peppers in a bowl. Cover with warm water and set aside to soak for 40 minutes. Drain and reserve the liquid.

2 Peel and chop the galanga. Finely slice the lemongrass and discard the top. Peel and mince the garlic and shallots. Wash, dry and chop the cilantro roots.

3 Roast the paprika, coriander, cumin seeds, turmeric and cinnamon together.

4 In a blender, combine the chili peppers and all the other ingredients. Purée until everything turns into a very smooth paste. If paste is too thick, thin with a little of the reserved hot pepper liquid.

5 This curry paste can be refrigerated in a clean jar for 4 to 6 weeks, or frozen in small portions in an ice-cube tray.

Chicken and peppers:

1	large onion, sliced	1
1	large red bell pepper, sliced	1
4 Tbsp.	peanut oil (or safflower, but not olive oil)	50 mL
4–10 Tbsp.	red curry paste	60–125 mL
1 14-oz. can	coconut milk	1 398-mL can
1 1/2 Tbsp.	fish sauce (or soy sauce)	25 mL
1 Tbsp.	brown sugar	15 mL
2 lb.	boneless chicken in 1-inch (2.5-cm) cubes	1 kg
Pinch	salt	Pinch
6	kaffir lime leaves, finely sliced	6
10 to 15	basil leaves, finely sliced	10 to 15

1 In an oiled wok, sauté the onion and red pepper for about 5 minutes. Set aside.

2 In the wok, add the peanut oil and fry the red curry paste on medium or high heat for 3 minutes. Add the coconut milk and bring to a boil. Add the fish sauce and brown sugar and boil for another 30 seconds.

3 Add the chicken and salt and cook for about 10 minutes on medium or high heat. Add the cooked onion mixture, kaffir lime leaves and basil and cook for another 5 minutes.

4 Serve with rice.

Thai Corn Patties with Sweet Chili Sauce

Sweet chili sauce:

	Vegetable oil	
1	medium onion, diced	1
1	red bell pepper, diced	1
8	cloves garlic, diced	8
2	fresh red chilies, finely diced (or dried chilies, soaked and diced)	2
1	chicken (or vegetable) bouillon cube, crushed	1
1/3 cup	brown sugar	75 mL
2 Tbsp.	fish sauce	25 mL
	Cornstarch (optional)	

1 In a medium frying pan, heat a little vegetable oil and sauté onion, red pepper, garlic and chilies until lightly browned.

2 In a blender, add two-thirds of the sautéed mixture and the bouillon cube, brown sugar and fish sauce and purée until smooth. Pour back onto the frying pan that has the sautéed mixture, add 2 Tbsp. (30 mL) oil and sauté for a couple of minutes. Add 2 cups (500 mL) of water and bring to a boil.

3 The texture and taste of this sauce can be varied by adding water or sugar or chilies or cornstarch. Mix 1 tablespoon (15 mL) cornstarch and 3 tablespoons (45 mL) cold water, stir into the sauce and bring to a boil).

Corn patties:

2 cups	corn kernels	500 mL
1 tsp.	roasted ground Szechwan peppercorns	5 mL
1 tsp.	fish sauce (or soy sauce)	5 mL
2 tsp.	garlic, minced	10 mL
2 tsp.	flour	10 mL
1	egg	1
1/4	cup cilantro, chopped	50 mL

Optional:

1 lb.	minced prawns (or minced chicken or minced pork)	500 g

1. In a blender, purée 1/2 cup (125 mL) of the corn kernels with a little water.

2. Combine the puréed corn with all the other ingredients and mix to form a thick batter.

3. In a skillet, heat a little oil and drop in batter 1 tablespoon (15 mL) at a time to form small patties. Fry until brown on one side, then turn over and brown the other side.

4. Serve with sweet chili sauce.

Pineapple Fried Rice

1	large fresh pineapple	1
1/4 cup	vegetable oil	50 mL
1	medium onion, chopped	1
2	cloves garlic, minced	2
1 cup	presoaked, sliced cloud ears (black fungus)	250 mL
4 cups	cooked rice	1 L
6 Tbsp.	fish sauce	75 mL
1 Tbsp.	sugar	15 mL
1/2 tsp.	white pepper	2 mL
2	green onions, sliced	2
1/4 cup	cilantro, sliced	50 mL

1 Cut the pineapple in half, from top to bottom, and hollow it out. Cut the pineapple flesh into cubes.

2 In a wok, heat the oil and stir fry the onion until soft, then add the garlic. With the heat on high, add cloud ears, pineapple cubes, rice, fish sauce, sugar and pepper. Mix thoroughly and cook until heated through. Add green onions and cilantro.

3 Serve in the hollowed-out pineapple shells.

Oregon Blue Pasta Salad

M ost years in February I go away somewhere hot to drink things with little umbrellas in them while Bill Richardson stays home in the cold and does the show. Thank you, Bill! While I was away one year, he talked to Ari Weinzweig, co-owner of Zingerman's Deli in Ann Arbor, Michigan, and got a million letters asking for this recipe, wouldn't you know.

3/4 lb.	Oregon blue cheese (or any high-quality blue cheese), crumbled	350 g
2 cups	mayonnaise	500 mL
2 Tbsp.	Dijon mustard	30 mL
1/2 Tbsp.	freshly ground black pepper	7 mL
1 lb.	good quality dried macaroni, cooked al dente	500 g
1/3 lb.	walnuts, toasted and coarsely chopped	150 g
1/4 lb.	carrots, grated	125 g
1/2 bunch	parsley, finely chopped	1/2 bunch

1 In a large mixing bowl, combine cheese, mayonnaise, Dijon mustard and pepper. Mix with a spoon, breaking up the large chunks of cheese.

2 Add pasta, walnuts and carrots. Mix thoroughly.

3 Place the salad in a big serving bowl and sprinkle parsley over the top as garnish.

Makes a large party-size batch.

Chakokhbili
(Chicken Stew with Herbs)

J ust around the time that Georgia began flexing its muscles against the Soviet state, Julianne Margvelashvili, author of a Georgian cookbook called The Classic Cuisine of Soviet Georgia: History, Traditions and Recipes, *came to talk about her life and her cooking. She married a Georgian and was smitten by the culture and cuisine, to say nothing of the fella. Please note her cautionary tale re the segmentation of a chicken.*

There is an oft-recounted old wives' tale in Georgia about the value of the bride being measured by her ability to cut a chicken into seventeen pieces, the exact number required for making good *chakokhbili*. If you're hoping to know whether you are the marrying kind, I suggest you begin practising: Try cutting eight pieces to begin with using the following recipe, and I'm sure you'll enjoy good *chakokhbili*. Worry about the remaining nine pieces and your mother-in-law next time.

Utskho suneli. Literally "a strange and fragrant smell from far away," this is an unfamiliar herb to us but one of the most popular in Georgia. I was able to identify it as *Trigonella cerulea* or European Blue White. The plant has no significant use beyond Georgia other than for animal fodder, although I have learned that it is also cultivated in Switzerland for use in flavouring sapsago cheese, breads and soups . . . Once the pale bluish purple flower appears, the plant is cut and hung to dry. The leaves are then crushed into a pale green powder with a wonderful aroma to which nothing can compare.

Marian Burros, food writer for the *New York Times* and beloved friend of many Georgians, searched diligently with me in 1988 to identify *utskho suneli*. We came to the conclusion that the closest substitute in our part of the world is powdered fenugreek petals, available in health-food shops and some specialty stores.

2–3 lb.	chicken	1–1.5 kg
2 Tbsp.	butter	30 mL
2	medium onions, finely chopped	2
1 cup	chicken stock	250 mL
4 to 6	potatoes, peeled and cubed	4 to 6
6	tomatoes, peeled and cubed	6
1 tsp.	Hungarian paprika	5 mL
2	cloves garlic	2
1	bay leaf	1
1 tsp.	dried coriander	5 mL
1 tsp.	powdered marigold petals	5 mL
1 tsp.	*utskho suneli*	5 mL
	Salt to taste	
2 Tbsp.	finely chopped parsley	30 mL
2 Tbsp.	finely chopped basil	30 mL
2 Tbsp.	finely chopped coriander	30 mL

1 Cut the chicken into serving pieces. Melt the butter in a frying pan and sauté the chicken until golden. Place in a 4-quart (4.5-L) casserole.

2 Add the onions to the frying pan and sauté until golden, then add to the chicken. Add the chicken stock and remaining ingredients except the fresh herbs.

3 Cover the casserole and simmer until tender, for about 25 to 30 minutes. Add half the chopped herbs and simmer 10 minutes longer. Serve garnished with the rest of the herbs.

Eggplant Orientale

This dish, which is often called Beggar's Caviar, originated in the Caucasus and has been popular in Russia for more than a century.

Eggplant sauce:

1	medium onion, sliced	1
2 oz.	peanut oil	50 mL
1 Tbsp.	garlic	15 mL
12-oz can	whole tomatoes, drained	1 398-mL can
12-oz. can	tomato purée	1 398-mL can
8 oz.	chili sauce	225 mL
1/2 tsp.	Tabasco	2 mL
	Salt and pepper to taste	
2 1-lb.	eggplants, peeled and cut into 1-inch (2.5-cm) cubes	2 500-g
1/4 cup	olive oil (or enough to coat the eggplant)	50 mL
1 Tbsp.	lemon juice	15 mL
1 quart	eggplant sauce	1 L
	Tabasco to taste	
	Salt and pepper to taste	
1 Tbsp.	fresh dill	15 mL

1. Eggplant sauce: In a large sauté pan or saucepan, gently sauté the onion in the peanut oil until translucent. Add the minced garlic, cooking an additional 2 minutes but not allowing it to brown. Add the remaining ingredients and simmer for 1 hour over moderate heat, stirring constantly. Reserve.

2. Preheat the oven to 350°F (180°C).

3. Place the cubed eggplant, olive oil and lemon juice in a large roasting pan and mix well. Bake for approximately 30 minutes, stirring every 10 to 15 minutes. Add the eggplant sauce to the roasted eggplant and bake an additional 30 minutes, or until the eggplant is tender. Allow to cool.

4. Chop the eggplant very fine or pulse in a food processor. Adjust the seasoning with Tabasco sauce and salt and pepper. Chill. Fold in the dill and serve slightly chilled.

5. To serve as a salad, garnish the plates with assorted lettuces and pickled vegetables. Serve with black bread.

Serves 6 or yields 2 quarts (2 L)

Chicken Kiev
(Cotelette à la Kiev)

Named after the queen city of Ukraine, Chicken Kiev is considered the pinnacle of Russian cooking. Financier Warren Buffet confides that since his first visit to the Russian Tea Room thirty years ago, he has eaten nothing but this dish. "It was great the first time I went in," he says, "so why try anything else?"

NOTE: The boneless chicken breasts sold in almost all supermarkets cannot be successfully used for this dish because of their small size. And supermarket chicken quarters, from which a breast with the attached wing bone necessary for this dish must be used, are almost always too small after boning. For a perfect Russian Tea Room Chicken Kiev, ask your butcher to cut the breasts from three 3 1/2-pound (1.6-kg) chickens and to leave the wing bones attached to the breasts. One whole boned, skinned and trimmed breast with 2 wing bones attached should weigh about 8 ounces (250 g). Or each halved breast, boned, skinned and trimmed, should weigh about 4 ounces (125 g). Chicken Kiev may be made with larger breasts, but this weight is easiest to handle.

Kiev butter:

2 Tbsp.	butter	30 mL
1	medium onion, minced	1
1 tsp.	garlic, minced	5 mL
1 cup	white wine	250 mL
1 tsp.	dried thyme	5 mL
1 tsp.	dried rosemary	5 mL
1 tsp.	marjoram	5 mL
2 tsp.	curry powder	10 mL
2 tsp.	paprika	10 mL
1/4 cup	cognac	50 mL
1/4 cup	Madeira	50 mL
1/4 cup	lemon juice	50 mL
1 Tbsp.	Worcestershire sauce	15 mL
1 lb.	softened sweet butter	500 g
1/2 cup	fresh chopped parsley	125 mL
1	egg yolk	1
	Salt and pepper to taste	

1 lb.	Kiev butter	500 g
3	double chicken breasts, wing bones attached; halved, skinned and boned (see note above)	3
	Salt and pepper to taste	
1	cup flour, for breading	250 mL
3	eggs, beaten	3
2	cups fine dry white bread crumbs	500 mL
2 quarts	cooking oil (or shortening)	2 L

1 To make Kiev butter: In a small stainless steel saucepan, melt 2 tablespoons (30 mL) of butter. Add the onion and cook until translucent. Do not let it colour. Add the garlic and sweat an additional minute; then add the white wine. Add the thyme, rosemary and marjoram. Reduce by three-quarters over moderate heat. Add the curry, paprika, cognac, Madeira, lemon juice and Worcestershire sauce and cook an additional 6 minutes. Remove from heat. Cool to room temperature and refrigerate.

2 Soften 1 pound (500 g) of sweet butter by paddling in a mixing bowl. Add half of the herb reduction (freeze the other half for later use) and the parsley to the butter and blend. Add the egg yolk and salt and pepper and mix until fully incorporated. Refrigerate until ready to use.

3 To prepare the Kievs: Preheat the oven to 350°F (180°C). Cut the butter into 6 equal pieces of about 2 tablespoons (30 mL) each. With your hands and the help of wax paper, shape each portion into a roll about 3 inches (7.5 cm) long and 3/4 inch (2 cm) thick. Wrap the butter portions in wax paper and freeze while preparing the chicken breasts.

4 Cut the wing tip from each breast half, leaving only the short bone that is attached to the meat to form a kind of handle. Scrape the skin and meat off this bone. With a cleaver or heavy knife, trim the joint neatly. Working carefully, cut this cleaned bone almost, but not entirely, loose from the breast half to which it is attached: the bone should hang from a thread of meat and sinew and be easy to twist. Lay the breast halves, smooth side down, on a cutting board and trim off any fat and gristle. With a small, sharp knife and the help of your fingers, carefully pull off the small fillet attached to each breast half. Lay the breast, smooth side down, and the fillet on a sheet of wax paper and cover both with another sheet of wax paper, allowing the bone and the part of the meat to which it is attached to stick out. With the flat side of a cleaver, a mallet or a rolling pin, pound the meat to a thickness of 1/8 inch (3 mm). Each pounded breast half will be approximately 8 inches (20 cm) long and 5 inches

(12.5 cm) wide. Each pounded fillet will be approximately 7 inches (18 cm) long and 9 inches (23 cm) wide. Pound the meat as thin as possible at the edges, since the thinner the edges, the easier it will be to seal them firmly to prevent butter from oozing out during cooking. Be careful not to tear the meat or to detach the bone from it.

5   To assemble the cutlets, gently peel off the wax paper from each breast half and fillet. Sprinkle evenly 1 side of each breast and fillet with 1/8 teaspoon (0.5 mL) each of salt and pepper. Place 1 portion of frozen butter in the centre of each breast half. Fold the wide side of the breast half lengthwise up over the butter; repeat with the other side. Fold the boneless end up over the butter. Twist the wing bone around and push the bone into the butter; only the 1/2-inch (1-cm) tip of the wing bone should be visible. Place the fillet shawl fashion around the bone and press it down tightly to adhere to the breast. It is essential to seal the butter in tightly or it will ooze out during cooking.

6   Coat each cutlet on all sides with flour, shaking off any excess. Dip lightly into beaten eggs, again shaking off any excess. Roll in bread crumbs, coating the cutlets evenly and yet again shaking off any excess. Place the cutlets in one layer on a platter and refrigerate for 1 to 2 hours.

7   Pour the oil in a large heavy saucepan or deep-fat fryer; the oil should reach 3 to 4 inches (7.5 to 10 cm) up the sides of the pan. Heat the oil until it registers 325°F (160°C) on a frying thermometer or until a 1-inch (2.5-cm) bread cube dropped into the hot oil turns golden in slightly less than 1 minute. Fry the cutlets, about 3 at a time, in the hot oil until golden brown. The cutlets should not touch each other during frying. Turn twice, using tongs or 2 spoons for turning and for removing the cutlets from the hot oil; this will prevent their being pierced. Drain on paper towels.

8   Transfer the golden brown Kievs to a baking dish and bake an additional 10 to 15 minutes. The Kievs should appear evenly coloured, and when they are held and shaken, one should feel the melted butter inside. The Kiev is very hot at this point, so use an oven mitt. Do not allow to overcook, or the butter will start to seep from the Kiev. Serve immediately on a bed of white rice with seasonal vegetables.

Serves 6.

Hot Pepper Risotto with Chèvre

Distinctive goat cheese and hot peppers give richness and zing to this creamy risotto. Outstanding with grilled lamb and roast chicken.

In order to make a great risotto, you must start with a thick, stubby Italian-style rice. The most common variety is Arborio. This rice can be purchased in Italian grocery stores, specialty food shops and supermarkets.

1/4 cup	butter	50 mL
1	onion, preferably Spanish, finely chopped	1
1	crushed garlic clove	1
1 1/2 cups	Arborio rice	375 mL
1/2 cup	dry white wine	125 mL
1/4–1/2 tsp.	dried hot pepper or chili flakes	1–2 mL
2 10-oz. cans	undiluted chicken broth	2 284-mL cans
2 cups	water	500 mL
1/2 cup	chèvre	125 mL
	Salt and freshly ground black pepper (optional)	

1 Melt the butter in a large wide saucepan. Add the onion and garlic and reduce heat to low. Sauté, stirring often, until the onion is soft, about 5 minutes. Then, add the rice and increase heat to medium. Stir the mixture until the rice is coated with butter.

2 Immediately add the wine while constantly stirring the rice mixture. Add 1/4 teaspoon (1 mL) chili flakes; if you like food extremely fiery, add 1/2 teaspoon (2 mL) and stir gently until the rice absorbs the wine.

3 Then, add the undiluted chicken broth and water, about 1/4 cup (50 mL) at a time. Stir constantly and wait until the liquid is absorbed before adding the next 1/4 cup (50 mL). This process is necessary in order to achieve the proper texture. Continue additions until all the liquid is absorbed and the rice is cooked, about 20 to 25 minutes. When cooked, the rice should be tender but not soft.

4 Stir in the cheese until evenly distributed. Taste and add salt and pepper, if needed.

Makes 4 servings.

I 've chosen this recipe from Monda's The New Chatelaine Cookbook *because it has three things I can't live without: hot peppers, goat cheese and garlic. The only trick to preparing risotto (aside from using Arborio rice) is that you have to stand there for 25 minutes and stir it. I always try to invite some youth with strong legs for risotto preparation.*

Venison Piquant

T wo or three times a year, the mob that works on the "Gabereau" show takes a luncheon or a dinner together. It's often a loud affair, with some participants (not I) actually dancing on the tables. A couple of times we have gone to the Kilimanjaro in Vancouver. Mr. Sunderji's eyes light up when he sees us coming; we've been known to buy many bottles of wine. He prepares a dandy venison dish native to East Africa. Maybe you could use lamb (or something that's game-y) if you can't find venison.

4.5 lb.	boneless leg of venison	2 kg
6	strips fatty bacon, thinly sliced	6
8	cloves	8
4	cloves of garlic, halved	4
12	peppercorns	12

Marinade:

1/3 cup	olive oil	75 mL
1 cup	red wine	250 mL
1	small onion, chopped	1
4	cloves garlic, finely chopped	4
1 tsp.	ginger root, finely chopped	5 mL
4	green chilies, seeded and chopped	4
2	cinnamon sticks	2
6	cardamom pods, pinched	6
1	small half-ripe papaya, chopped Seeds of the papaya	1
1/2 bunch	basil, chopped	1/2 bunch
1/2 bunch	green coriander, chopped	1/2 bunch
4	bay leaves	4

2 Tbsp.	sweet mango (or fruit) chutney	30 mL
4	green onions, sliced	4
1 tsp.	Spanish paprika Cornstarch	5 mL

2	chopped green onions	2
3	medium mangoes, peeled and sliced	3

1 To prepare the roast: Lay the meat flat on a board and tenderize with a mallet. Thread the bacon strips through meat at regular intervals. Prick meat evenly with cloves, garlic and peppercorns. Place in a flat container.

2 To prepare the marinade: In a wok or skillet, heat 2 tablespoons of the olive oil and sauté onions until tender. Add garlic, ginger, chilies, cinnamon and cardamom. Stir for a minute more. Add rest of the ingredients and heat through. Do not boil.

3 Drizzle the meat with the marinade. Cover and let stand in the refrigerator for 24 to 48 hours, the longer the better. Turn over the meat at convenient intervals.

4 Preheat oven to 325°F (160°C).

5 Remove meat from marinade; reserve marinade. Brush the chutney on the meat, and sprinkle with the sliced green onions. Roll up the meat and secure it with fasteners.

6 Place meat in an ovenproof dish and pour the marinade over the meat. Cover tightly and bake for about 3 hours. Time will vary, depending on the age of the deer (ask your butcher). Remove the meat from oven and keep it warm.

7 Skim the fat from the drippings. Remove the bay leaves and papaya seeds. Deglaze the pan with a little more wine if necessary. Add paprika and heat. Thicken with cornstarch and water to desired consistency.

8 Cut the roast into medallions and pour the sauce over it. Garnish with chopped green onions and something red.

9 Serve with wild or brown rice and sliced mangoes.

Coconut and Lime Truffles

reg Hook is more than just a chocolate maker; he actually produces edible art. He even reproduces, in chocolate, miniature versions of the works of the famed Haida artist and sculptor Robert Davidson. A few select restaurants and hotels in Vancouver present these chocolate art replicas to their guests.

Mr. Hook graciously supplied a couple of his recipes for making your own fancy chocolates at home. This way the rest of Canada can enjoy their slimming qualities.

For the chocolate, Vahlrona is the best, but any imported Belgian or Swiss chocolate will do.

1 1/2 lb.	white chocolate	750 g
3/4 cup	whipping cream	200 mL
1/4	vanilla bean, split open and seeded	1/4
6 Tbsp.	coconut milk	100 mL
1	lime, juiced and strained	1
	Toasted coconut	

1 Bring a pot of water to boil and remove from heat.

2 Put the chocolate in a heatproof bowl and set over the pot. (Chocolate burns very easily.) Stir occasionally until melted.

3 In another pot, bring whipping cream to boil with the vanilla bean. When it has boiled, take it off the heat. Add the coconut milk and remove the vanilla bean. Pour this onto the chocolate and mix well. Add the lime juice and stir well. Cover with plastic film and refrigerate overnight.

4 Use a melon baller to scoop out rounds and roll them in the toasted coconut. These will need to be kept refrigerated or they will become too soft. They can also be kept frozen (tightly wrapped) and served from the freezer. They take only a short time to thaw.

GREG HOOK, OWNER, CHOCOLATE ARTS STORE, VANCOUVER

Dark Chocolate Truffles

1 lb.	dark chocolate	500 g
3/4 cup	whipping cream	200 mL
2 Tbsp.	liqueur of choice (or to taste)	25 mL
	Cocoa or chopped nuts (optional)	

1 Follow steps 1 to 3 in the recipe for Coconut and Lime Truffles.

2 Use a melon baller to scoop out rounds and roll them in cocoa powder. If you find the cocoa too bitter, add some icing sugar to the cocoa powder.

3 These truffles can also be rolled in nuts, but they should then be frozen. If refrigerated, the nuts will absorb moisture and become soggy.

Kahlua Coffee Liqueur

I never met Todd Wilbur. I never saw the completed book, but he sure was funny on the radio. At first, you might think this is a chap who doesn't have enough to do, that he can spend day in and day out trying to figure out how to make a Big Mac in his own kitchen. Who cares when you can get one for a couple of bucks down the road? But price is not the issue—his pursuit was two-fold: one, it drove him crazy that people knew things he didn't; and two, he wanted to see if he could re-create some of these popular items without benefit of chemical additives. It seems he was quite successful with the twinkie, not a mile off from Kentucky fried chicken, and there were dozens of others, all in Top Secret Recipes: Creating Kitchen Clones of America's Favorite Brand-Name Foods. In this case, you get Kahlua, which Mr. Wilbur says is the largest-selling liqueur in America.

You will need an empty 26 oz. (750-mL) liquor bottle with a screw top or a bottle with a resealable lid for storing the liqueur.

It is very important that you used a covered saucepan when making this drink. The alcohol will boil away if the solution is not covered when it gets hot.

Also, the longer this drink is bottled and stored in a dark, cool place, the better it will taste. For the best flavour, store it for at least 30 days before drinking. Probably the hardest part of making this simple recipe is not drinking the stuff before it matures!

2 cups	80-proof vodka	500 mL
2 cups	water	500 mL
1 1/4 cups	granulated sugar	300 mL
5 tsp.	vanilla extract	25 mL
5 tsp.	instant coffee	25 mL

1 Combine all of the ingredients in a saucepan. Cover and cook over medium heat, stirring occasionally, until the sugar has completely dissolved.

2 Remove the mixture from the heat and let it cool. Be sure to keep it covered.

3 Store in an empty 26-oz. (750-mL) liquor bottle with a screw top and let it mature for at least 30 days.

Makes 26 oz. (750 mL).

HOUSEHOLD HINTS

To get grease and oil off your hands, mix a handful of granulated sugar with a dollop of dish soap and scrub thoroughly.
—MAURO AZZANO OF RICHMOND, B.C.

Tony Aspler's Punch

Tony Aspler used to be a radio producer, but he pressed on to become a wine expert and a novelist, two things that all CBC producers long to become. One of his books is intriguingly titled Blood Is Thicker Than Beaujolais.

It's been reported to me that Mr. Aspler throws a pretty good party. No doubt the guests are served this recipe—they don't call it punch for nothing!

Essence of cloves is difficult to find, so steep 5 cloves in the Curaçao or its equivalent for a few hours. Then remove the cloves and discard them.

The Burgundy could be, for example, Macon Supérieur by Bouchard.

2	egg yolks at room temperature	2
1 oz.	liquid honey	30 mL
1 oz.	Curaçao, not the blue kind (or Triple Sec or Grand Marnier)	30 mL
	Essence of cloves	
1 pint	Burgundy, heated to just under boiling	500 mL

1 Using a whisk, mix the egg yolks until creamy. Add the liquid honey and mix.

2 Add the Curaçao to the eggs and mix.

3 Very slowly and a very little at a time, add the hot wine to the egg mixture, stirring constantly.

4 Serve in cups rather than wine glasses.

Festive Christmas Stollen

I f you were to look in my kitchen cupboard, you would find all the ingredients for Caren's Christmas stollen—they've been there for over a year. I made the stollen with Caren (at Caren's Cooking School— Great Culinary Adventures Inc. in Vancouver) but I've never had the nerve to try making it on my own. It's an equipment crisis: every time I go to the store, I look at those mix masters— the ones with the bread hooks—and I say, "I really should have one of those things." But then I think of the generations of people, women mostly, who made a perfectly beautiful stollen before electricity, and I'm stuck. I still haven't made another— but you can (with or without a mix master).

2 tsp.	sugar	10 mL
1 cup	warm water	250 mL
2 Tbsp.	Fermipan yeast (2 8-g pkg.)	30 mL
1 cup	scalded milk	250 mL
1/2 cup	unsalted butter, melted	125 mL
1/2 cup	sugar	125 mL
1 tsp.	salt	5 mL
6 cups	all-purpose unbleached flour	1.5 L
1/4 tsp.	ground mace	1 mL
1/4 tsp.	ground nutmeg	1 mL
2	large eggs, beaten	2
	Grated rind of 1 lemon	
1/2 cup	currants, soaked in 1/2 cup (125 mL) brandy	125 mL
1/2 cup	candied peel	125 mL
1/2 cup	dried apricots, chopped	125 mL
1/2 cup	raisins, soaked in 1/2 cup (125 mL) rum	125 mL
1/2 cup	almonds, chopped	125 mL
	Confectioner's sugar	

1 Stir 2 teaspoons (10 mL) of sugar into the warm water, sprinkle over the yeast and let it proof. Set aside.

2 To the scalded milk, add the butter, sugar and salt. Cool to lukewarm.

3 In a large bowl, combine 3 cups (750 mL) of the flour, mace and nutmeg. Add the milk mixture and the yeast. Stir to create a thick batter. Add the eggs and lemon rind.

4 Mix in the dried fruit and almonds. Add the remaining flour, 1 cup (250 mL) at a time. Knead the dough continuously for about 10 minutes, until you have a nice smooth elastic dough. If the dough is still sticky, knead in more flour.

5 Place the dough in a buttered bowl and let it rise in a draft-free area for about 1 1/2 hours, or until doubled in bulk.

6 Punch down and shape into wreaths, stollens or braids. Let them rise again for an addition 1 to 1 1/2 hours, or until doubled in bulk.

7 Preheat oven to 350°F (180°C). Bake for 40 minutes. Dust with confectioner's sugar.

Panforte de Siena

L esley Stowe is the proprietor of a Vancouver establishment that purveys fine foods. You know, one of these places where you find virgin saffron, if there is such a thing— exclusive and perfect products. But she's a down-to-earth woman, and she loves to cook. This is a type of cookie from Siena, mostly served at Christmas, but who cares!

1/2 cup	hazelnuts	125 mL
1/2 cup	blanched almonds, coarsely chopped	125 mL
1 cup	candied peel, finely chopped	250 mL
1/4 cup	unsweetened cocoa powder	50 mL
1/2 cup	all-purpose flour	125 mL
1/2 tsp.	ground cinnamon	2 mL
1/4 tsp.	grated nutmeg	1 mL
1/2 cup	sugar	125 mL
1/2 cup	honey	125 mL

Topping:

| 2 Tbsp. | icing sugar | 30 mL |
| 1 tsp. | ground cinnamon | 5 mL |

1 Preheat oven to 375°F (190°C).

2 Spread the hazelnuts on a cookie sheet and place in the oven for 5 to 10 minutes. Remove from oven and turn down to 300°F (150°C). Rub the nuts in a clean cloth to remove the skins, then chop coarsely.

3 In a bowl, combine the hazelnuts, almonds, candied peel, cocoa, flour, cinnamon and nutmeg. Stir well.

4 In a saucepan, combine the sugar and honey. Heat gently until the sugar dissolves. Bring to a boil until the sugar thermometer registers 240°F (115°C), the soft ball stage. Take off the heat, add to the nut mixture, and stir well.

5 Turn out into an 8-inch (20-cm) flan ring lined with parchment paper. Spread flat, making sure the mixture is an even 1 inch (2.5 cm) thick.

6 Bake for 30 to 35 minutes. Turn out onto a wire rack, peel off the paper, and leave to cool.

7 Topping: Sift together the icing sugar and cinnamon. Sprinkle over the panforte. Serve cut into small wedges.

Bûche de Noël

It is possible that Thierry Damilano (né France) is the most athletically courageous person I've met. He climbs things, like mountains and cliffs and walls of ice. He also windsurfs for hours and hours at a time. He cooks with roughly the same bravado at his restaurant in Vancouver, unusually called Chez Thierry.

On Bastille Day, the restaurant is the scene of excitement as M. Damilano doesn't just uncork champagne, he sabres the bottle, while attired in full French revolutionary regalia, including a splendid tricorn hat. The patrons love the show, as do passers-by, who often appear somewhat shocked as the corks go whizzing by. Occasionally, a table of diners will break into some section of La Marseillaise. *All quite rousing.*

Preparation time: 1 hour
Baking time: 10 to 12 minutes
Baking temperature: medium
Serves 6 people

Ingredients for the cake:

3	eggs (separated)
100 gr	butter
150 gr	sugar
50 gr	cornstarch
30 gr	flour

Ingredients for the chocolate cream filling:

50 gr	baking chocolate
2 spsp	cold espresso coffee
4	egg yolks
6 spsp	sugar
150 gr	butter
2 spsp	rum
12	crushed pralines (sugar-coated almonds)

Ingredients for the coffee cream garniture:

2	egg yolks
3 spsp	sugar
100 gr	butter
2 spsp	rum
2 spsp	cold espresso coffee
1 spsp	cold instant coffee

Marzipan flowers and meringue mushrooms to decorate

HOUSEHOLD HINTS
To keep cookies like hermits and chocolate chips from going stale, add a slice of peeled, raw potato to the cookie jar or tin. You can also use a slice of apple instead, but some apples with strong flavours will affect the flavour of the cookies.

—BELLE RAFUSE
OF HALIFAX, NOVA SCOTIA

Batter preparation:
With a wooden spatula blend the egg yolks, butter and 2/3 of the sugar until consistency is white and foamy. Gradually add small amounts of cornstarch and flour to thicken. Beat egg whites with the remaining sugar until stiff. Lightly add the two mixtures together.

Pour batter into a pregreased rectangular baking dish until 1 inch thick and bake for 10 to 12 minutes.

Chocolate cream filling preparation:
Break the chocolate into a small saucepan and melt it in a bain-marie with the espresso coffee, until pastelike in consistency. In a separate bowl, mix the egg yolks and sugar until thick and foamy. To melt the butter, warm a terrine with hot water. Work the butter slowly in the terrine until it is soft. Add the egg mixture, the chocolate-coffee paste and the rum to the melted butter.

Coffee cream garniture preparation:
Beat the egg yolks and sugar until thick and foamy. To melt the butter, warm a terrine with hot water. Work the butter slowly in the terrine until it is soft. Add the egg mixture, the rum, the espresso and the instant coffee to the melted butter.

Making the cake:
Remove the baked cake from the oven and allow to cool between two damp cloths. Flatten it and cover with the chocolate cream mixture. Sprinkle the pralines on top and proceed to roll the cake tightly into a "log." Once rolled, cut both ends at an angle and keep the cut pieces separate. Cover the "bûche" and the ends with the coffee cream mixture. Using a fork, drag the prongs lengthwise along the cake to create a barklike effect. Do the same to each of the two cut ends, and place them alongside of the log to create branches. Add the marzipan and meringue decorations and keep the cake in a cool place until ready to serve.

Joyeux Noël et bon appétit!

The recipe included here was aired at Christmas time in 1989. It is an elaborate, somewhat complicated and beautiful thing. We present the recipe here unedited and unchanged; the measurements and instructions come from Thierry's own computer. I wish you some luck.

P.S. I think "spsp" means soupspoon, and "gr" means gram(s).

Victorian Dark Christmas Cake

In 1980 I somehow managed to get the job of summer fill-in for Don Harron, who was then the host of "Morningside" on CBC Radio. I was green in ability and colour, and quite frankly the stories given me were often well beyond my scope. That is a really polite way to say it.

Fortunately, relief came my way in the form of the great chef, caterer and writer Peter Cochrane of Ottawa. He came into the studio in Toronto with giant pots and pans and prepared a summer lunch. It was so much fun I almost forgot I was on the radio, which was a relief to all concerned. Many years later, I'm still talking and Peter is still cooking.

1 cup	butter	250 mL
1 cup	brown sugar	250 mL
6	eggs, separated	6
2 cups	all-purpose flour	500 mL
1 tsp.	cinnamon	5 mL
1 tsp.	allspice	5 mL
1 tsp.	nutmeg	5 mL
1 tsp.	baking soda	5 mL
1 tsp.	salt	5 mL
1/2 cup	brandy (or rum or whisky)	125 mL
1/2 cup	molasses	125 mL
1/4 cup	buttermilk	50 mL
1 1/2 cups	raisins	375 mL
1 1/2 cups	currants	375 mL
1 1/2 cups	almonds, blanched and slivered	375 mL
1 1/2 cups	candied citron (or other candied peel)	375 mL
1 1/2 cups	candied cherries, halved	375 mL

1 Preheat oven to 300°F (150°C).

2 In a large bowl, cream together the butter and sugar until light in colour. Add the egg yolks one by one, beating them well into the mixture.

3 In a medium bowl, sift together 1 1/2 cups (375 mL) of the flour with the cinnamon, allspice, nutmeg, baking soda and salt.

4 In a small bowl, mix the brandy, molasses and buttermilk. Add to the butter mixture alternately with the sifted dry ingredients.

5 In a large bowl, mix the 1/2 cup (125 mL) of reserved flour with the raisins, currants, almonds, citron and cherries. Stir them well into the batter.

6 Beat the egg whites until they hold a peak but are not dry. Fold into the batter.

7 Line a cake tin with several layers of wax paper and spoon the batter into it. Put a shallow pan of water in the bottom of the oven while you are baking the cake. Bake for two to three hours, checking for doneness with a cake tester.

3

Cross-Canada Recipe Contest Winners

The Great Gabereau Meat Loaf Contest

The first year of the annual recipe contest, we didn't exactly have the system down pat. Nor were we sure how many Canadians actually cared for or prepared meat loaf. Or how many recipes would use mushroom soup or ketchup (many of them did, by the way, but we didn't hold that against them). We were quite surprised when bags of mail suddenly began to appear, all full of recipes for little rectangular slabs of ground meat pressed into a pan.

We spread the recipes all over the floor in the office, stared at them for quite a while, pushed them around a bit, and came to some sort of piling system. After days of shouting, pushing and piling, five were chosen to be prepared. Joan Athey of the CBC publicity department drew the short straw; we went to her house and proceeded to wreck her kitchen.

The show's crew was divided into teams. I was with Evan Stewart, and our preparation won. Maybe we cheated. Maybe we added a bit more garlic. I can't remember for sure. The judges (Jurgen Gothe, host of CBC Stereo's "Disc Drive" and Bob Robertson and Linda Cullen from "Double Exposure") voted unanimously for the Italian Meat Loaf submitted by Taiya Barss from Cape Breton.

HOUSEHOLD HINTS

To peel boiled eggs more easily, add a little vinegar to the water before cooking them.

—SHARRI BROWNE
OF FORT NELSON, B.C.

Italian Meat Loaf

1 Tbsp.	olive oil	15 mL
1/2 lb.	mushrooms, sliced	250 g
2 lbs.	lean hamburger	1 kg
1 lb.	ground pork	500 g
1/2 lb.	frozen spinach, cooked, squeezed dry and finely chopped	250 g
1	egg, beaten	1
2 cups	soft bread crumbs	500 mL
1/2 cup	provolone cheese, in 1/4-inch (5-mm) cubes	125 mL
2	cloves garlic, crushed	2
1/2 cup	red wine	125 mL
4 Tbsp.	grated Parmesan cheese	60 mL
1 cup	ham, cut into 1/2-inch (1-cm) cubes	250 mL
2 tsp.	oregano	10 mL
1 tsp.	basil	5 mL
2 tsp.	salt	10 mL
1/2 tsp.	black pepper	2 mL

1 Preheat oven to 375°F (190°C).

2 In a small skillet, heat the oil and sauté mushrooms.

3 In a large bowl, mix everything well. Put into 2 bread pans and bake in oven for 1 hour. If you don't want a crusty top, cover the pans with foil.

Fiesta Meat Loaf

2	eggs	2
1 cup	well-drained canned crushed pineapple	250 mL
1/4 cup	chili sauce	50 mL
1/4 tsp.	garlic salt	1 mL
	Freshly ground black pepper	
1 cup	fine dry bread crumbs	250 mL
1	small onion, finely chopped	1
1 1/2 lbs.	regular ground beef	750 g
1/2 lb.	sausage meat 250 g	

Glaze (optional):

1/2 cup	ketchup	125 mL
1/4 cup	brown sugar	50 mL

1 Preheat oven to 350°F (180°C).

2 In a large bowl, beat eggs and stir in crushed pineapple, chili sauce, garlic salt and pepper. Add bread crumbs, onion, ground beef and sausage meat, mixing thoroughly by hand.

3 Line a 9 x 5-inch (23 x 13-cm) pan with perforated foil (to let fat escape). Press the meat into the pan.

4 To make the glaze: Mix together ketchup and brown sugar and brush half of the mixture over the loaf. Brush on the remaining glaze when the loaf is well on the way.

5 Put the pan in the oven for about 1 1/2 hours. If you are glazing the meat loaf, cover with foil until the second glaze is brushed on. Let loaf "drip" for a few minutes before serving.

Variations

Instead of sausage meat, use chopped cooked sausages.

Instead of crushed pineapple, use finely chopped apple.

Danish Meat Loaf

1 lb.	lean ground beef	500 g
1 lb.	lean ground pork (or veal or chicken)	500 g
1 cup	cracker crumbs (or fine bread crumbs)	250 mL
1	large onion, chopped	1
1	large green pepper, chopped	1
1	large red pepper, chopped	1
2	small zucchini, cut in cubes with skin on	2
1 cup	Havarti cheese, cubed	250 mL
	Salt and pepper to taste	
	Table cream	

1 Preheat oven to 350°F (180°C).

2 In a large bowl, mix together all the ingredients. Add enough table cream so the mixture holds together.

3 Press into a loaf pan and bake for 45 to 60 minutes or until done.

My Meat Loaf

4	slices dryish bread, crusts and all	4
	Salt and pepper to taste	
	Sage, thyme and savoury to taste	
2–3 Tbsp.	butter	30–45 mL
1	small onion, chopped	1
1/3 cup	warm water	75 mL
1–1 1/2 lbs.	ground beef	500–750 g
1	egg (optional)	1

Topping:

1/2 cup	ketchup	125 mL
2 tsp.	brown sugar (or jam or jelly)	10 mL
1 tsp.	mustard powder (or any kind of mustard)	5 mL
1/2 tsp.	nutmeg	2 mL

1 Preheat oven to 350°F (180°C). If you're using a glass pan, preheat to 325°F (160°C).

2 Break up the bread slices into roughly 1/2-inch (1-cm) pieces and place in a large bowl. Season the bread cubes with salt, pepper and your favourite amounts of sage, thyme and savoury.

3 In a saucepan, melt the butter and simmer the onion in it until limp. Add the warm water. Sprinkle over the bread and toss with a fork until evenly moisturized.

4 Add the ground beef and egg (optional—use if you want a firm, solid loaf). Mix well (hands are best). Place in a lightly greased 9 x 5-inch (23 x 13-cm) loaf pan, and make a trench down the middle to hold the topping, leaving a little wall at each end as sort of a dam to contain it.

5 Topping: Mix together the ketchup, brown sugar, mustard and nutmeg. Pour into the trench in the meat loaf, using a knife to spread a little of it over the rest of the loaf as a glaze. Bake for 1 1/2 hours.

Variations
The meat loaf can be extended to serve more people by adding more stuffing and/or leftover vegetables, including potatoes. I sometimes add a bit of horseradish to perk up the taste or put more chopped onion in the stuffing. The main thing is to distribute everything well in the mixing.

Creole Meat Loaf

Creole sauce:

3 Tbsp.	butter	45 mL
1	onion, chopped	1
2	cloves garlic, finely chopped	2
1	green pepper, finely chopped	1
1	red pepper, finely chopped	1
3 Tbsp.	flour	45 mL
1 1/2 cups	milk	375 mL
1/3 cup	hot chili sauce	75 mL
2 Tbsp.	tomato paste	30 mL
1 tsp.	salt	5 mL
1 tsp.	Worcestershire sauce	5 mL

Meat loaf:

1 1/2 lbs.	lean ground beef	750 g
1	egg	1
1/2 cup	fine bread crumbs	125 mL
1/2 tsp.	salt	2 mL
1/4 tsp.	black pepper	1 mL
1 tsp.	basil	5 mL
1/4 tsp.	dry mustard	1 mL

Mushroom sauce:

1/2 cup	milk	125 mL
1/2 cup	mushrooms, sliced	125 mL

1. Preheat oven to 400°F (200°C).

2 In a large frying pan, heat butter and sauté onion, garlic, green and red peppers until vegetables are soft.

3 Sprinkle with the flour and cook 1 minute. Whisk in milk. Cook for 5 minutes on high heat until the mixture is boiling; stir occasionally. Add chili sauce, tomato paste, salt and Worcestershire sauce. Cook 5 minutes longer, stirring occasionally.

4 In a large bowl, combine ground beef, egg, bread crumbs, salt, pepper, basil, mustard and 1/2 cup (125 mL) of the creole sauce. Shape the mixture into a loaf and place in a loaf pan. Spoon 1/2 cup (125 mL) of the creole sauce on top of the loaf. Bake for 45 to 50 minutes.

5 Mushroom sauce: In the meantime, add milk and mushrooms to the remaining creole sauce in the saucepan and simmer on low until the loaf is ready.

6 To serve, slice the meat loaf and pour mushroom sauce over the slices.

The "In a Stew" Contest

Things picked up even more in year two of the annual recipe contest. People got excited by the prospect of real prizes—pottery made by B.C. artists, for example; plus my long-out-of-print book, and maybe even a beer with Bill Richardson if they ever came to Vancouver.

We went for stew in '90, and this time we cooked in my kitchen. Again, the crew split up into teams, and hey, guess what? My team won again. But the winning recipe turned out to be somewhat controversial. It called for an entire jar of peanut butter, smooth or crunchy. That turned out to be quite a bit.

Perhaps I did something wrong that made it a bit gluey, sort of wallpaper paste–like. One guy said the finished product looked like a stewed muppet in a pot. But somehow I managed to convince the judges, who thought it was splendid. The judges this time were Eve Johnson, food writer for the Vancouver Sun, Guus Mostart, the artistic director of the Vancouver Opera, and Canada's greatest living actor, Nicola Cavendish.

HOUSEHOLD HINTS
To rid your fingers of odours from cooking preparations, scrub with a cola drink.
—ALEX ELMSLEY
OF KELOWNA, B.C.

Groundnut Stew

3 Tbsp.	peanut oil	45 mL
2	large onions, chopped	2
2	large cloves garlic, crushed	2
2 lbs.	stewing beef (or cubed steak)	1 kg
	Salt and pepper to taste	
1 16-oz. jar	peanut butter (smooth or crunchy)	1 500-g jar
	Ground hot red pepper to taste	
	Hot cooked rice (white or brown)	
4	hard-boiled eggs	4

1 In a large skillet, heat the peanut oil and fry the onion and garlic until just tender. Add the meat and brown. Add 2 cups (500 mL) of water, salt and pepper. On low heat, cook the meat till tender. Add peanut butter. Add hot pepper to your own heat level.

2 Serve stew on a bed of hot rice. Garnish with the hard-boiled eggs.

Winter Root Stew

Roasted vegetables:

4	small potatoes	4
2	yams	2
4	carrots	4
2	small onions	2
2	small white turnips (or parsnips)	2
1	head fennel	1
2	heads garlic, left whole	2
1/2 cup	safflo	125 mL
1/2 cup	olive oil	125 mL

Vegetable stock:

4	carrots	4
2	leeks	2
2	celery sticks (or heart)	2
2	medium onions, speared with cloves	2
4	shallots	4
4	cloves garlic	4
10 to 15	black peppercorns	10 to 15
	Parsley stems	
1	bay leaf	1
	Thyme	
1/4 cup	flour	50 mL
	Salt and pepper to taste	

1 Preheat oven to 400°F (200°C).

2 Roasted vegetables: Peel or scrub well all the vegetables and cut them up so the pieces are the same size, as close to whole as possible. Coat well with the safflo and olive oil. Place in a flat roasting tray and put in oven for 1 hour. Check on them periodically and turn so they remain crisp on the outside and do not stick to pan.

3 Vegetable stock: Peel and chop the vegetables and garlic. Place in a stock pot and cover with 4 cups (1 L) of water. Add peppercorns and herbs. Simmer for 45 minutes, skimming the top if a film should appear. Strain and return to the stock pot.

4 Remove roasted vegetables and sprinkle 1/4 cup (50 mL) flour into the pan drippings. Heat and slowly add some stock to make a sauce. Bring sauce to a boil as though you were making gravy. Remove skins from roasted heads of garlic and add the garlic to the sauce, which should be thick enough to coat the back of a spoon. (Any leftover stock can be frozen.) Put the roasted vegetables in the stock pot with the sauce and heat for 10 to 15 minutes. Season to taste.

Lamb Cranberry Stew

1/4 cup	salad oil	50 mL
2.2 lbs.	boneless lamb shoulder, cubed	1 kg
2 tsp.	salt	10 mL
1/4 tsp.	crushed thyme	1 mL
4	whole cloves	4
1 Tbsp.	lemon juice	15 mL
1	clove garlic, halved	1
1 10-oz. can	condensed beef bouillon	1 284-mL can
1	medium onion,	sliced 1
5	medium carrots, quartered	5
1 cup	whole-berry cranberry sauce	250 mL
2 Tbsp.	cornstarch	30 mL
1 can	potatoes, drained	1 can

1 In a dutch oven or heavy kettle, heat oil and brown lamb. Add salt, thyme, cloves, lemon juice, garlic, bouillon, onion and 1 cup (250 mL) of water. Cover and bring to boil. Reduce heat and simmer for 45 minutes.

2 Add carrots, cranberry sauce and more water if needed. Cover and simmer 35 to 45 minutes or until lamb and carrots are tender.

3 Dissolve cornstarch in 1/4 cup (50 mL) of water and add to the stew with the potatoes. Cook, stirring, just till thickened.

Sauerkraut Stew

2–3 Tbsp.	oil	30–45 mL
1 lb.	pork shoulder, cubed	500 g
1	large onion, chopped	1
1 tsp.	caraway seeds	5 mL
1 Tbsp.	paprika powder	15 mL
1 tsp.	salt (optional)	5 mL
1/2 cup	hot water	125 mL
1 lb.	sauerkraut	500 g
1 tsp.	flour	5 mL
1 cup	sour cream	250 mL

1 In a large skillet, heat oil and brown meat. Add onion and sauté until light brown. Add caraway, paprika, salt, water and sauerkraut. Simmer for 45 minutes or until the meat is done.

2 Mix the flour into the sour cream. Stir into the stew.

Beef Stew in Cranberry Chutney

2 Tbsp.	vegetable oil	30 mL
1 1/2 lbs.	stewing beef, trimmed of fat and cubed	750 g
1	large onion, chopped	1
1	stalk celery with leaves, chopped	1
1	clove garlic, minced	1
1 1/4 cups	boiling water	300 mL
2 cups	cranberries	500 mL
1/2 cup	raisins	125 mL
1/4 cup	walnuts (optional)	50 mL
1 Tbsp.	cider vinegar	15 mL
1 Tbsp.	honey	15 mL
1/4 tsp.	ground cinnamon	1 mL
1/4 tsp.	ground ginger	1 mL
1/4 tsp.	ground cloves	1 mL
	Cayenne pepper to taste	

1 In a large skillet, heat oil. Add beef and brown on all sides. Add onions and celery, sauté until golden brown. Add garlic and sauté mixture 1 minute, stirring constantly (do not let garlic change colour). Stir in boiling water, then add the remaining ingredients.

2 Cover and simmer for 1 1/4 hours or until beef is tender and liquid is reduced to 1/3 or 1/2 cup (75 or 125 mL). If pan juice gets low during cooking, add a little hot water. If juice does not reduce, uncover skillet during the last 30 minutes of cooking and stir often. Season to taste.

The Muffin Contest

By the third year, we knew we were onto something. People were asking, "When's the contest? When's the contest?" So '91 became the year of the muffin. Linda Meinhardt, a champion baker, knows her muffins—she owns the Bread Garden restaurant and bakery in Vancouver. We asked her to come to the studio to kick off the muffin search. Her launching recipe follows.

You'll be surprised to know that thousands of recipes appeared, but mercifully a system had been developed by producer Sheila Peacock (files—that kind of thing).

Ms. Meinhardt was particularly smitten by one of the runners-up, the Five-Star Muffins. She decided to modify it slightly and prepare it for her restaurant-bakery, the Bread Garden, and put my name on it. Time passed, and my daughter, who had lived away from Vancouver for some years, returned home. Innocently, she went to the Bread Garden and was amazed to see her name on a piece of cardboard stuck in a muffin. "What is that?!" she asked the youthful attendant. "It's a woman who works on the radio who makes these all the time," he replied. "I know who she is," my daugher said, "but I've never seen her bake a muffin in my life!" My cover was blown.

HOUSEHOLD HINTS

For baby diaper rash, sprinkle cornstarch on the baby's behind instead of baby powder.
—CARMEN LAVIGNE OF MONTREAL, QUEBEC

Bread Garden
Basic Muffin Recipe

6 cups	wholewheat flour	1.5 L
6 cups	all-purpose flour	1.5 L
4 cups	brown sugar	1 L
2 Tbsp.	baking soda	30 mL
2 Tbsp.	baking powder	30 mL
1 tsp.	salt	5 mL
1 1/2 tsp.	nutmeg	7 mL
1 1/2 tsp.	cinnamon	7 mL
1 1/2 tsp.	allspice	7 mL
2 cups	vegetable oil	500 mL
6	medium whole eggs	6
2 Tbsp.	vanilla	30 mL
4 cups	buttermilk	1 L
7 cups	fruit (berries or cut-up fruit)	1.75 L

1 Preheat oven to 375°F (190°C).

2 In a large bowl, combine all the dry ingredients, mixing by hand or with a spatula.

3 In a medium bowl, combine all the wet ingredients, whisking gently.

4 Add liquid mixture to the dry mixture and mix by hand or with a spatula until well blended. Do *not* use a mixer.

5 Add fruit and mix until well distributed.

6 Put muffin cups into muffin pans. Scoop the dough into the muffin cups. Bake for 25 minutes or until golden brown.

Makes 36 muffins.

Rhubarb Pecan Muffins

2 cups	all-purpose flour	500 mL
3/4 cup	sugar	175 mL
1 1/2 tsp.	baking powder	7 mL
1/2 tsp.	baking soda	2 mL
1 tsp.	salt	5 mL
3/4 cup	chopped pecans	175 mL
1	large egg	1
1/4 cup	vegetable oil	50 mL
2 tsp.	grated orange peel	10 mL
3/4 cup	orange juice	175 mL
1 1/4 cups	fresh rhubarb, finely chopped	300 mL

1 Preheat oven to 350°F (180°C).

2 In a large bowl, combine the flour, sugar, baking powder, baking soda, salt and pecans.

3 In a medium bowl, beat egg. Stir in oil, orange peel and juice. Add to flour all at once and stir just until batter is moist. Stir in the rhubarb.

4 Lightly grease large 2 3/4 x 1 1/2-inch (7 x 4-cm) muffin cups and fill three-quarters full. Bake for 25 to 30 minutes.

Makes 12 muffins.

Cornmeal Strawberry Muffins

1 1/2 cups	all-purpose flour	375 mL
1 1/2 cups	cornmeal	375 mL
1/2 cup	sugar	125 mL
3 tsp.	baking powder	15 mL
1 tsp.	baking soda	5 mL
1/2 tsp	salt	2 mL
2	large eggs	2
1 cup	milk	250 mL
1/4 cup	vegetable oil	50 mL
1 cup	unsweetened frozen strawberries, thawed and sliced	250 mL

1 Preheat oven to 375°F (190°C).

2 In a large bowl, combine flour, cornmeal, sugar, baking powder, baking soda and salt.

3 In a medium bowl, beat eggs well. Stir in milk, oil and strawberries.

4 Make a well in the dry ingredients and add the egg mixture all at once, stirring just until combined.

5 Lightly grease large 2 3/4 x 1 1/2-inch (7 x 4-cm) muffin cups and fill three-quarters full. Bake for 20 minutes.

Makes 14 muffins.

Georgina's Oat Bran Muffins

3	large egg whites	3
3/4 cup	brown sugar	175 mL
1/3 cup	extra light olive oil	75 mL
1/2 cup	fancy molasses	125 mL
4 tsp.	baking powder	20 mL
4 tsp.	baking soda	20 mL
1 1/4 tsp.	ground cinnamon	6 mL
1 tsp.	ground nutmeg	5 mL
1/2 tsp.	ground cloves	2 mL
1/2 tsp	salt	2 mL
4 1/2 cups	skim milk	1.125 L
4 1/2	cups oat bran	1.125 L
2 cups	stone-ground wholewheat flour	500 mL
1/2 cup	raisins, soaked and drained	125 mL
1 cup	raw unsalted sunflower seeds	250 mL
3 cups	carrots, finely chopped (using a food processor)	750 mL
2 cups	grated zucchini	500 mL

1 Preheat oven to 400°F (200°C).

2 In a large bowl, lightly beat egg whites and sugar. Add oil, molasses, baking powder, baking soda, cinnamon, nutmeg, cloves, salt and milk. Mix well. Add oat bran and flour and mix. Add remaining ingredients and stir to blend. Batter will be thin.

3 Lightly grease large 2 3/4 x 1 1/2-inch (7 x 4-cm) muffin cups and fill to the top with batter. Bake for about 30 minutes.

Makes about 24 muffins.

Nichol Vineyard's Five-Star Muffins

1/2 cup	raisins	125 mL
3/4 cup	dates, chopped	175 mL
1 1/2 cups	wholewheat flour	375 mL
1 cup	large flake oats	250 mL
1/2 cup	wheat germ	125 mL
1 cup	natural bran	250 mL
2 tsp.	baking powder	10 mL
1 tsp.	baking soda	5 mL
1	small apple, cored and finely chopped	1
1/3 cup	chocolate chips	75 mL
1/2 cup	medium, unsweetened coconut	125 mL
1	orange, cut in pieces	1
1/2 cup	undrained, canned crushed pineapple	125 mL
1	ripe banana, sliced	1
1/2 cup	vegetable oil	125 mL
2	large eggs	2
1 cup	apple juice (or pineapple juice)	250 mL

1 Preheat oven to 375°F (190°C).

2 In a small saucepan, combine raisins, dates and 1/4 cup (50 mL) water. Simmer over medium heat until mushy (add more water if necessary). Set aside.

3 In a large mixing bowl, combine flour, oats, wheat germ, bran, baking powder and baking soda. Add chopped apple, chocolate chips and coconut.

4 In a blender, combine raisin mixture, orange, pineapple, banana, oil, eggs and apple juice. Blend until puréed.

5 Make a well in the dry ingredients and pour in puréed mixture. Stir until just blended.

6 Lightly grease large 2 3/4 x 1 1/2-inch (7 x 4-cm) muffin cups and fill to the top with batter. Bake for about 18 to 20 minutes or until done.

Makes 18 to 20 muffins.

YEAR FOUR

The Pasta Sauce Search Contest

I have to say that all of the recipe contests have been great events filled with fun, laughter, jumping up and down, good food, good company—a productive excuse for a party. Too bad that you all couldn't be there. But the day that the national pasta sauce search unfolded, it was evident (to me at least) that it was going to be very Italian indeed. The judges were the ones who really caused all the commotion this time. They were Bruno Gerussi, actor and former cooking show host; Diana Leong, cooking teacher, Vancouver Chinatown guide and French teacher; and Umberto Menghi, an Italian guy who owns a lot of restaurants including Il Giardino, a hot spot in Vancouver. He gave us a recipe to launch the contest.

I ought to point out that this was the very first year that wine became part of the equation. Things got livelier and livelier until Umberto had completely covered his beautiful pearlescent silk shirt with tomato sauce. At first, Diana was a bit shy (who could blame her?), but with Bruno singing and all, she felt more relaxed. At some point Bruno and Umberto were shouting and singing and spilling everything. But amidst the chaos we managed to choose a winner, which wasn't easy because they were all first-rate, just like the judges.

Spaghetti Scottadito

Sauce:

3 tsp.	extra virgin olive oil	15 mL
4	cloves garlic	4
2 cups	tomatoes, skinned, seeded and chopped	500 mL
1/2 cup	basil, finely chopped	125 mL
	Salt and pepper to taste	
1/2 cup	Parmesan cheese, freshly grated	125 mL
1 lb.	spaghetti	500 g

1 In a large pan, heat oil and sauté garlic cloves on each side until golden. Add tomatoes and cook at medium heat for 4 minutes (or until tomatoes are soft but not mushy). Add basil and cook for another 2 minutes. Season with salt and pepper to taste.

2 Cook pasta al dente: 3 to 5 minutes for fresh pasta, 5 to 7 minutes for dried.

3 Add cooked pasta to sauce in pan and toss for 2 minutes to mix the pasta and sauce. Add Parmesan cheese and serve.

Serves 4.

Variation

If you like it spicy, add chopped red jalapeño peppers.

Neapolitan Tomato Sauce

Instead of the Unico ground tomatoes, purée added, as specified below, Primo tomatoes can be used. If "purée added" is not available, add 1/2 small can of tomato paste. The ground tomatoes are a must because other types have too much water in them.

2 Tbsp.	dried basil (fresh if possible)	30 mL
3 1-inch	chili peppers (optional)	3 2.5-cm
1/4 cup	olive oil	50 mL
3 medium	cooking onions, chopped	3 medium
3	cloves or more thinly sliced garlic	3
1 can	Unico ground tomatoes, purée added	1 can
1 tsp.	salt	5 mL
	Freshly grated Parmesan (or Romano) cheese	

1 If using dried basil, grind up to free the flavour and set aside.

2 In a small saucepan, combine the chili peppers with 1 1/2 cups (375 mL) water. Cover the pot and cook at a slow boil until the chili flavour has gone into the water, about 30 minutes. Set aside.

3 In a heavy-bottomed saucepan, combine olive oil, 1/3 cup (75 mL) of water and onions. Place on high heat and stir so that onions do not stick or burn. When the water has evaporated, reduce heat and continue cooking the onions until transparent and limp, about 3 to 4 minutes. If onions start to burn, reduce heat and cook for a longer period of time.

4 Once onions are cooked, add garlic and cook for another 30 to 60 seconds. Reduce heat to a simmer, add the ground tomatoes, salt and basil. Cook on low for 15 to 20 minutes to blend flavours, stirring occasionally. If the sauce boils, the basil and garlic flavours will be lost, so keep heat low.

5 Taste the sauce. If a hot sauce is desired, add cooked chili water bit by bit to taste. This method controls the hotness of the sauce without surprising errors.

6 Serve the sauce over hot pasta and sprinkle with freshly ground Parmesan or Romano cheese.

Aglio Modenese

1/2 cup	olive oil	125 mL
4	cloves garlic, sliced	4
3 to 4	fresh mint leaves	3 to 4
	Salt to taste	
	Freshly grated Parmesan cheese	

1 In a frying pan, heat oil and sauté garlic until it is partially browned and sizzling. Add mint leaves and turn off heat. Sprinkle on salt to taste.

2 Serve the sauce over hot spaghetti, toss and add cheese to taste.

Grandma Castle's Spaghetti Sauce

2 Tbsp.	butter	30 mL
1/2 tsp.	salt	2 mL
4	large cooking onions, chopped fine	4
1 lb.	lean ground beef	500 g
1 sm can	tomato paste (plus two cans water)	1 sm can
1 med can	tomatoes	1 med can
1 med can	tomato juice	1 med can
6 or 7	whole allspice cloves, crushed (or powdered allspice to taste)	6 or 7
1	garlic clove, crushed	1
2	bay leaves	2
1 tsp.	oregano	5 mL
3 Tbsp.	sugar (or less to taste)	45 mL
1 small	hot pepper, minced (or a sprinkle of cayenne pepper)	1 small
	Salt and pepper to taste	
	Grated Parmesan cheese	

1 In a frying pan, heat butter and salt, add onions and sauté until soft. Add ground beef and sauté thoroughly. Add the rest of the ingredients and simmer slowly for 2 1/2 to 3 hours or until thick.

2 Before removing the sauce from the stove, add a generous sprinkling of Parmesan cheese.

Perfect Salmon Pasta

1 cup	green peas (fresh preferred)	250 mL
1 1/2 cups	cream	375 mL
1/2 tsp.	grated lemon rind	2 mL
4 oz.	Nova Scotia (or other) smoked salmon, thinly sliced	125 g
	Slivers of sun-dried tomatoes	
	Freshly grated Parmesan cheese	

1 In a saucepan, simmer peas in cream until cooked. Add lemon rind and smoked salmon. Heat thoroughly.

2 Serve on your favourite cooked pasta, garnished with slivers of sun-dried tomatoes and Parmesan cheese.

Serves 2.

The Condiment Recipe Contest

Do you remember that bit in the movie The Graduate when the guy says to the Dustin Hoffman character, "Plastics, my boy, plastics—that's where the future is"? Well, I had a similar experience with a friend of mine who said, "Condiments, my dear, condiments. The future is in condiments." He was right, and if I had invested then in what I now know to be true, I could have been the condiment queen. Because condiments are indeed the thing. I can't get enough of them.

So that's why, in year five, I invited Joe Zallen of Que Pasa Mexican Foods in Vancouver to come in to the studio to talk about the salsa phenomenon. He gave us a recipe to start things off and was also a condiment contest judge, along with Caren McSherry-Valagao, owner of Caren's Cooking Company, and Sal Ferreras, percussionist, performer and condiment lover. Surprisingly, we got only a few ketchup recipes, though, as expected, most of the 300 or so entries were of the savoury variety. I didn't cook—and by now, I wasn't even allowed to be a judge. I was systematically being shut out of my own game, but I still got to pour the wine.

Pico de Gallo

3	fresh jalapeño peppers, finely chopped	3
4 to 5	Roma tomatoes (or 1 large steak tomato), diced	4 to 5
1	small red onion, diced	1
3	cloves garlic, minced	3
1 tsp.	salt	5 mL
1 tsp.	dried red chili, crushed (Pequin or Caribe, optional)	5 mL
3 Tbsp.	fresh cilantro, chopped	45 mL
	Garnish of lime (or lemon) wedge	

1 Combine all the ingredients and allow to marinate and develop natural juices for at least 1 hour. Chill before serving. Garnish with wedge of lime or lemon.

"Bug" Mustard

1/3 cup	flour	75 mL
1/4 cup	sugar	50 mL
1/4 cup	or more Keen's dry mustard	50 mL
1/3 cup	olive oil	75 mL
3/4 cup	vinegar	175 mL
1/2 tsp.	dried chili peppers	2 mL
1/2 tsp.	or more pimento, chopped	2 mL
1/4 tsp.	cayenne pepper	1 mL
	Pinch of salt	
	Freshly ground black pepper	
	Paprika	

A note about the winning recipe for "Bug" Mustard. This is quite a runny condiment, so don't be shocked. We have had quite a few letters and phone calls about the consistency and whether or not it's right. It is, and don't fight it. Also, the flour is not cooked; but if you can't stand that idea, experiment.

1 In a bowl, combine flour, sugar, mustard and olive oil. Slowly add the vinegar, mixing until smooth. Add chili, pimento and cayenne, mixing well. Add salt, pepper and paprika to taste.

HOUSEHOLD HINTS

To get fleas out of your carpet, liberally sprinkle borax all over it. Vacuum as usual. Repeat every couple of days for at least three weeks. This will kill fleas in the larval stage and won't harm people or pets.

—SHEILA ANDERSON OF LITTLE FORT, B.C.

Al-Zahawiq (Yemeni Hot Sauce)

3	cloves garlic	3
1 tsp.	cumin	5 mL
1/2 tsp.	salt	2 mL
3 tsp.	ground coriander	15 mL
6	fresh jalapeño peppers	6
2	tomatoes, chopped	2
	Juice of 1 lemon (or lime)	
1/2 tsp.	sugar	2 mL
1/4 cup	water	50 mL

1 In blender, combine all the ingredients and liquidize. Pour into a saucepan and bring to the boil. Cool.

2 Serve with bread as a dip, or as a sauce with pasta, potatoes or meat.

English Mint Chutney

3 cups	vinegar	750 mL
2 cups	brown sugar	500 mL
3 tsp.	mustard	15 mL
2 tsp.	salt	10 mL
1/2 lb.	ripe tomatoes, skinned	250 g
1 lb.	sour apples (about 2 1/2 to 3 apples)	500 g
6	onions	6
1 1/2 cups	seedless raisins	375 mL
2	sweet green peppers, seeded	2
1	red pepper, seeded	1
1/2 cup	mint leaves	125 mL
2 Tbsp.	lemon juice	30 mL

1 In a saucepan, combine the vinegar, sugar, mustard and salt, and heat. Cool thoroughly.

2 Chop very fine the tomatoes, apples, onions, raisins, green and red peppers and mint leaves. Mix in a large bowl and add lemon juice. Add the cold vinegar mixture and stir thoroughly.

3 Place in cold sterilized jars and seal.

Cold Eggplant Condiment

1	large eggplant	1
3/4 cup	olive oil	175 mL
3	onions, thinly sliced	3
1	green pepper, thinly sliced	1
1 1/4 cups	celery, diced	300 mL
1 28-oz.	Italian plum tomatoes,	1 798-mL
can	drained and chopped	can
1 Tbsp.	capers	15 mL
1 Tbsp.	pine nuts	15 mL
1/4 cup	green Italian olives, chopped	50 mL
1/2 cup	red wine vinegar	125 mL
2 Tbsp.	sugar	30 mL
3/4 tsp.	salt	4 mL
	Grinding of black pepper	
1 Tbsp.	tomato paste (optional)	15 mL

1 Peel eggplant and cut into 1-inch (2.5-cm) cubes. In a frying pan, heat olive oil and sauté eggplant until very soft. Remove and drain.

2 Add onions to frying pan, using more oil as necessary, and sauté until soft. Add green pepper and sauté until limp.

3 Return eggplant to the pan. Add celery and tomatoes. Simmer for 20 minutes. Add capers, pine nuts and olives.

4 In a saucepan, heat vinegar and dissolve sugar, salt and pepper over low heat. Add the vegetable mixture. Cover and simmer on lowest heat for 30 minutes. If you like it thick, add tomato paste.

5 Serve at room temperature or cold.

Traveller's Salsa

8	large Roma tomatoes	8
1/2	small green pepper	1/2
1/2	large red pepper	1/2
3	green onions	3
1/2 cup	red onion	125 mL
2	fresh jalapeño peppers	2
1 Tbsp.	parsley	15 mL
2	cloves garlic	2
1/4 tsp.	oregano	1 mL
1/4 cup	canned hot pickled jalapeño peppers, drained	50 mL
2 Tbsp.	juice from canned hot pickled jalapeño peppers	30 mL

1 Dice tomatoes into 1/4-inch (5-mm) cubes. Chop the rest of the ingredients finely.

2 Combine all ingredients and refrigerate. Allow to sit for at least 2 hours before serving. If the salsa is not juicy enough for your liking, refrigerate for one day before serving to permit juices to form.

The Family Favourites Contest

Six times lucky! I can't imagine what we'll do next. Family favourites was an easy idea to agree on. It had a well-rounded feel—a beginning, a middle and an end. We liked that.

Entries arrived by the truckload for the biggest contest response ever. Actor Jackson Davies, cheerful and unknowing, agreed to launch the contest with his Peanut Butter and Banana Pancakes, but he didn't get off that easily. He was cajoled (possibly conned) into being a chef and a judge. The other judges were Monda Rosenberg, food editor of Chatelaine magazine, and Mark Davidson, wine instructor and sommelier of the William Tell Restaurant in Vancouver.

Mark brought the wine, all Canadian, all great—all gone. Jackson said he had never had thirty-five glasses of wine in one afternoon before. Monda was modest in her intake, and Mark is used to it. We had six semi-finalists, two from each category, and we ate it all. That works out to be two whole meals each. They were all great, but the dessert with bourbon really won our hearts.

Peanut Butter and Banana Pancakes

I think that Saturday mornings are the best time to be a kid. I know that it is at our house, because that's the morning the kids get to go downstairs to the TV room and watch their favourite cartoons while I make one of my many culinary masterpieces, Peanut Butter and Banana Pancakes. It's really quite easy to make. Just use whatever pancake mix that you usually use. I grew up in Alberta, so I use Coyote pancake mix. All you do is add mashed-up bananas and a couple of dobs of peanut butter to the mix. These pancakes go great with "Teenage Mutant Ninja Turtles" or old "Beachcombers" reruns.

1 cup	pancake mix	250 mL
1 cup	milk (or water)	250 mL
1	egg (optional)	1
1 Tbsp.	sugar (optional)	15 mL
2 Tbsp.	vegetable oil	30 mL
1	banana, peeled and mashed	1
2 dobs	peanut butter	2 dobs

1 Preheat griddle. If electric, set at 400°F (200°C).

2 Place all the ingredients in a bowl. Stir until batter is fairly smooth.

3 Spoon batter onto hot, lightly greased griddle. Turn pancakes when tops are covered with bubbles and edges look cooked. Turn only once.

Makes 12 to 14 4-inch (10-cm) pancakes.

Bourbon Sauce Date Pudding

N ancy's eighty-six-year-old mother, Theresa (Trix) Bates, has made this recipe for special winter dinners ever since Nancy can remember. Trix got it from her sister, Mary E. Hehir McGrath, who died in 1992 at the age of ninety-six, so it must be good for you. The family does not know anything about its origins but has always assumed that it came from the Deep South, perhaps New Orleans.

The pudding and sauce keep well, covered, in the refrigerator. Just heat the sauce again to serve.

Date pudding:

1 1/4 cups	flour	300 mL
1/4 tsp.	baking powder	1 mL
1/4 tsp.	salt	1 mL
1 cup	chopped pecans	250 mL
1 8-oz. pkg.	dates	1 227-g pkg.
1 tsp.	baking soda	5 mL
1 cup	boiling water	250 mL
1/4 cup	butter	50 mL
1 cup	sugar	250 mL
1	egg	1

Bourbon sauce:

2 cups	sugar	500 mL
1 Tbsp.	butter	15 mL
1 tsp.	vanilla (or 1 1/2 oz./45 mL bourbon, rum, sherry)	5 mL
	Whipped cream	

1 To make the pudding: Sift flour into a bowl and mix with baking powder and salt. Add pecans and mix.

2 Cut dates into thumbnail-size pieces with *wet* kitchen scissors. Place in a small bowl, add baking soda and mix. Pour boiling water over the dates. Let stand until cool.

3 In a separate bowl, cream butter and sugar well. Add egg and beat well.

4 Combine flour and sugar mixtures. Add date mixture and stir in.

5 Pour the batter into a lightly greased 8 x 12-inch (20 x 30-cm) pan. Smooth the top. Bake at 300°F (150°C) for one hour, until a toothpick comes out clean when inserted. Remove from oven and set aside.

6 To make the sauce: In a saucepan, combine the sugar and 1 cup (250 mL) water until sugar dissolves. Bring to a boil and cook for 5 minutes. Remove from heat and stir in the butter and vanilla (or bourbon, rum, sherry).

7 Serve squares of pudding cool or warm with hot sauce and whipped cream.

Thai Fish Soup

P atricia got this recipe from her sister in Toronto. It was the first Thai recipe she ever made, and now it's a favourite, particularly with the vegetarians in the family.

2 Tbsp.	vegetable oil	30 mL
1	leek, cut into julienne strips	1
3	cloves garlic, minced	3
1 Tbsp.	ginger root, minced	15 mL
1/4 tsp.	red-hot pepper flakes	1 mL
1 Tbsp.	curry powder	15 mL
1 tsp.	grated lemon peel	5 mL
1	red pepper, cut into strips	1
1 cup	canned coconut milk	250 mL
1 cup	canned puréed plum tomatoes and juice	250 mL
2 Tbsp.	soy sauce	30 mL
2 Tbsp.	lemon juice	30 mL
1/2 lb.	cleaned shrimp, sliced in half	250 g
1/2 lb.	scallops	250 g
1 lb.	white fish fillets (halibut)	500 g
1/4 cup	fresh cilantro, chopped	50 mL
2 Tbsp.	fresh basil, chopped	30 mL
2 Tbsp.	fresh mint, chopped	30 mL
2 Tbsp.	fresh chives, chopped	30 mL

1 In a large saucepan, heat oil. Add leek, garlic, ginger and pepper flakes. Cook for a few minutes but do not brown. Add curry powder and cook for 30 to 60 seconds.

2 Add lemon peel, red pepper, coconut milk and tomatoes. Bring to a boil. Add soy sauce, lemon juice and 3 cups (750 mL) water. Bring back to a boil, then simmer gently for 15 minutes.

3 Add shrimp, scallops and fish. Cook gently for 5 minutes or until fish is just cooked. Taste and adjust seasoning if necessary.

4 Mix cilantro, basil, mint and chives together. Place equal amounts of the mixed herbs in each individual soup bowl. Pour soup over the herbs and serve immediately.

Makes 6 to 8 servings.

Poulet Diable Blanc

Due to its economy, ease and delicious taste, this recipe has been "done to death" by Catherine's family for some thirty years. It's the recipe that launched Catherine and her three siblings into entertaining. Her youngest brother made reference to it during his wedding speech, saying that to receive an invitation to the wedding, a guest had to have eaten Poulet Diable Blanc, prepared by him, at least three times.

Originally, this recipe came from the Cookbook of the Shirley Cripps Home for Crippled Children in Southern Rhodesia, circa 1960. Catherine's father was posted to Rhodesia for three years and her mother was a volunteer at the home when the cookbook was put together.

1	chicken, roasted and still warm (or buy a hot roasted bird at a delicatessen)	1
1/2 pint	whipping cream	250 mL
2 dessert spoons	soy sauce	2 dessert spoons
2 dessert spoons	Worcestershire sauce	2 dessert spoons
2 dessert spoons	Dijon mustard	2 dessert spoons

1 Cut up chicken into serving pieces (thighs, drumsticks, etc.).

2 Whip the whipping cream. Stir in soy sauce, Worcestershire sauce and Dijon mustard. Spread mixture over warm chicken pieces.

3 Place coated chicken pieces in a single layer in a baking dish. Bake at 350° F (180°C) for 20 minutes or until the coating is "tacky-ish."

Oyster Mushroom and Pine Nut Pâté

3 cups	oyster mushrooms	750 mL
1 cup	dry vermouth	250 mL
4 Tbsp.	butter	60 mL
1 cup	pine nuts	250 mL
1	large clove garlic	1
2/3 cup	Parmesan cheese, freshly grated	150 mL
2 Tbsp.	dry sherry	30 mL
2	green onions, minced	2
2 Tbsp.	parsley, minced	30 mL
1 Tbsp.	whipping cream	15 mL
	Salt and pepper to taste	

1 In a large frying pan, simmer the mushrooms in the vermouth, covered, for 5 minutes.

2 In a small frying pan, heat the butter and lightly brown the pine nuts.

3 In a blender or food processor, purée the mushrooms, pine nuts and the rest of the ingredients until smooth. If necessary (especially if using a blender), add additional vermouth, 1 tablespoon (15 mL) at a time, to create a spreadable mixture that the blender can blend.

4 Serve with crackers and thin slices of baguette.

Jennifer developed this recipe herself when her then eight-year-old daughter developed a taste for oyster mushrooms and she found a market vendor who had drastically marked down a large number of not-quite-perfect specimens. It makes a big batch and is a party as well as a family favourite. This pâté can also be frozen.

Bill Kry's Tuna Casserole
As Adapted by His Son Ed Kry

I n Ed's teens, he secretly watched his father (Bill) make this family comfort casserole and month by month learned to recreate it himself. He urged us to destroy his recipe if it didn't make the finals, because for over twenty-five years friends and family have begged for it and Ed has refused. Now the secret is out, and it's with great pride that Ed has named it for his dad.

2	medium-size cooking onions, chopped small (pea size)	2
2	stalks celery, diced same size as onions	2
1	red pepper, diced same size as onions	1
1	green pepper, diced same size as onions	1
1 cup	chopped mushrooms	250 mL
2 cups	white rice	500 mL
2 sm tins	of tuna in water, drained	2 sm tins
	Salt and pepper to taste	
2 cups	croutons	500 mL
1 can	cream of mushroom soup	1 can
1/2 cup	milk (skim if you want)	125 mL
	A pinch or two of nutmeg	
	A bottle of Worcestershire sauce	

1 Sauté onions until transparent. Reserve.

2 Sauté celery until just soft. Reserve.

3 Sauté red and green peppers until just soft. Reserve.

4 Sauté mushrooms until soft. Reserve.

5 Make the rice, using 2 cups (500 mL) rice, 4 cups (1 L) of water, a bit of salt; don't peek. Reserve.

6 In an ovenproof casserole bowl:
—layer about 1/3 of the rice
—sprinkle in 1/2 of the tuna, onions, celery, peppers and
  mushrooms, in layers
—salt and pepper to taste
—layer another 1/3 of the rice
—layer the rest of the tuna, onions, celery, peppers and
  mushrooms as before
—layer the last of the rice
—layer the croutons on top
—mix the cream of mushroom soup with the milk and
  drizzle on top of croutons
—sprinkle with a pinch or two of nutmeg

7 Put uncovered into a 325°F (160°C) oven for half an hour
or until golden on top.

8 Serve sloppily with a big spoon, so all the ingredients
mix in every mouthful.

9 Splash a bit of Worcestershire sauce on your serving.
Stand back and accept the praise.

(If no one is looking, you can microwave the vegetables
instead of sautéeing them.)

Acorn Squash Dessert

W here did Martha find this recipe? Where she finds all her recipes—in her head. She has been making it for about thirty years, and people love it.

2	small acorn squash	2
8 Tbsp.	brown sugar	120 mL
1/2 cup	raspberries, fresh or frozen	125 mL
1 pint	vanilla ice cream, slightly softened	500 mL
4 Tbsp.	cherry liqueur	60 mL
	Whipped cream	
	Shredded chocolate	

1 Preheat oven to 350°F (180°C).

2 Trim ends off squash and cut in half. Scoop out seeds. Put 2 tablespoons (30 mL) brown sugar into each half.

3 Set each half in foil. Twist loosely at top and leave a small opening for steam to escape. Place in a baking dish and bake for 1 hour. Cool. The squash halves may be served warm or cold.

4 Swirl the raspberries into the slightly softened ice cream. Drop one large scoop into each squash half.

5 Dribble 1 tablespoon (15 mL) of cherry liqueur over the ice cream in each half. Top with whipped cream. Sprinkle a small amount of shredded chocolate over top. Serve.

Makes 4 servings.

Acknowledgements

T hank you to all the cooks, without whose talents this book would not have been possible. Not only that, but all the recipe contest winners, guest chefs, organizations, and cookbook authors (and their publishers) all generously gave us permission to reprint their recipes.

James Barber, Shepherd's Pie from *Ginger Tea Makes Friends*, copyright © 1971 by James Barber, reprinted by permission of the author. Evelyn Birkby, Magnificent Chicken Pie, Carrot Biscuits, Real Country Biscuits from *Up a Country Lane Cookbook* by Evelyn Birkby, reprinted by permission of the University of Iowa Press. Bob Blumer, Chez Bob's Caesar Salad from *The Surreal Gourmet* by Bob Blumer copyright © 1992, published by Chronicle Books, reprinted by permission. Cherie Calbom and Maureen Keane, Ginger Ale, Garden Salad Special, Hair Growth Cocktail from *Juicing for Life* by Cherie Calbom and Maureen Keane © 1992, $12.95, published by Avery Publishing Group, Inc., Garden City Park, New York, (800) 548-5757, reprinted by permission. The Clever Cleaver Brothers, Shrimp Dijonaise from *Cookin' with the Cleavers*, copyright © 1990 by Casslee Corporation d/b/a Clever Cleaver Productions, courtesy of The Clever Cleaver Brothers® at Clever Cleaver Productions, San Diego, California, and by permission of Wynwood House, a division of Baker Book House Co. Kirsten Dixon, Smoked Salmon Cardamom Spread from *The Riversong Lodge Cookbook* by Kirsten Dixon, reprinted by permission of Alaska Northwest Books. Carol Ferguson and Margaret Fraser, Flapper Pie from *A Century of Canadian Home Cooking* by Carol Ferguson and Margaret Fraser, 1992, published by Prentice-Hall Canada Inc., reprinted by permission of the publisher and authors. Bette Hagman, Rice-Ricotta Pancakes from *The Gluten-Free Gourmet* by Bette Hagman, copyright © 1990 by Bette Hagman, reprinted by permission of Henry Holt and Company, Inc. Ted Hancock, Gold Strike from *The Canadian Honey Recipe Book*, edited by Terry Huxter, by permission of the publisher, British Columbia

Index

K

L

M